2nd EDITION

Textbook 3

T0340480

Series editor and author: Peter Clarke

William Collins' dream of knowledge for all began with the publication of his first book in 1819.

A self-educated mill worker, he not only enriched millions of lives, but also founded a flourishing publishing house. Today, staying true to this spirit, Collins books are packed with inspiration, innovation and practical expertise.

They place you at the centre of a world of possibility and give you exactly what you need to explore it.

Collins. Freedom to teach.

Published by Collins

An imprint of HarperCollins*Publishers*
The News Building, 1 London Bridge Street, London,
SE1 9GF, UK

HarperCollins*Publishers*
Macken House, 39/40 Mayor Street Upper, Dublin 1,
D01 C9W8, Ireland

> Browse the complete Collins catalogue at
> **collins.co.uk**

ISBN 978-0-00-861374-7

British Library Cataloguing-in-Publication Data

A catalogue record for this publication is available from the British Library.

Series editor: Peter Clarke
Author: Peter Clarke
Product manager: Holly Woolnough
Editorial assistant: Nalisha Vansia
Copy editor: Tanya Solomons
Proofreader: Catherine Dakin
Illustrator: Ann Paganuzzi
Cover designer: Amparo Barrera
Cover illustrator: Amparo Barrera
Internal designer: 2Hoots Publishing Services
Typesetter: David Jimenez
Production controller: Alhady Ali
Printed and bound in Great Britain by Martins the Printers

> Busy Ant Maths 2nd edition components are compatible with the 1st edition of Busy Ant Maths.

This book is produced from independently certified FSC™ paper to ensure responsible forest management.

For more information visit: harpercollins.co.uk/green

Acknowledgements

p54t Fresher/Shutterstock; p63tr Sockagphoto/Shutterstock.

Contents

Multiplication and division

Fractions

Year 3 Number facts

How to use this book

This book shows different pictures, models and images (representations) to explain important mathematical ideas to do with number.

At the start of each double page is a brief description of the key mathematical ideas.

The key words related to the mathematical ideas are shown in **colour**. It's important that you understand what each of these words mean.

The main part of each double page explains the mathematical ideas. It might include pictures, models or an example.

Your teacher will talk to you about the images on the pages.

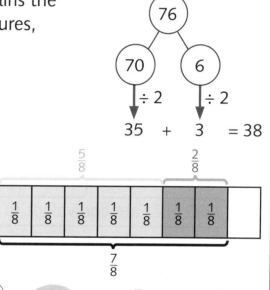

100s	10s	1s
100 100 100	10 10	1 1 1 1 1 1 1
100 100 100 100	10 10 10 10 10	1 1 1 1 1 1 1 1

Sometimes there might be questions to think about or an activity to do.

Pages 6-7

This refers to mathematical ideas on other pages that you need to understand before learning about the ideas on these two pages.

Pages 10-11, 14-17, 20-43

This refers to mathematical ideas on other pages that use or build upon the ideas on these two pages.

This helps you think more deeply about the mathematical ideas.

Use the pages in this book to help you answer the questions in the Pupil Books.

Numbers to 1,000

A 3-digit number is made of hundreds (100s), tens (10s) and ones (1s). 1 hundred is the same as 10 tens or 100 ones.

Look at the Base 10.

Count in steps of 10. How many steps did you count?

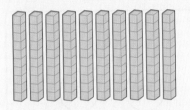 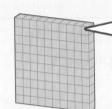

How many ones make 100?

The Base 10 show that 10 tens **is equal to** 100, and 100 ones is equal to 100.

We can also say that:

10 tens are **equivalent** to 100.

100 ones are equivalent to 100.

Look at the chart below. It is called a Gattegno chart.

It shows ones, tens and **hundreds**.

What patterns do you notice?

How are the rows the same? How are they different?

What happens in each column of numbers?

We call the numbers in this row **multiples of 10**.

The numbers in this row are called **multiples of 100**.

100	200	300	400	500	600	700	800	900
10	20	30	40	50	60	70	80	90
1	2	3	4	5	6	7	8	9

Look at these ten frames and Base 10.

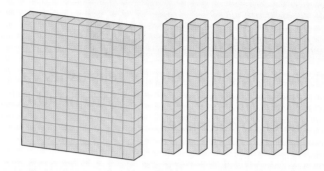

The ten frames and Base 10 both show that 16 tens is equal to 160.

We can also say that: 16 tens are equivalent to 160.

Find 160 on this number grid.

All the numbers on this grid are multiples of 10.

What patterns do you notice?

How are the rows the same?

How are they different?

What happens in each column of numbers?

10	20	30	40	50	60	70	80	90	100
110	120	130	140	150	160	170	180	190	200
210	220	230	240	250	260	270	280	290	300
310	320	330	340	350	360	370	380	390	400
410	420	430	440	450	460	470	480	490	500
510	520	530	540	550	560	570	580	590	600
610	620	630	640	650	660	670	680	690	700
710	720	730	740	750	760	770	780	790	800
810	820	830	840	850	860	870	880	890	900
910	920	930	940	950	960	970	980	990	1,000

Say Point to a number on the grid and say how many tens it is made from.

Look at this place value chart.

100s	10s	1s
		5
	5	0
5	0	0

50 (5 tens) is ten times 5 ones.

500 (5 **hundreds**) is one hundred times 5 ones.

500 (5 **hundreds**) is ten times 50 (5 tens).

The zeros are **place holders**. They change the **value** of 5.

Pages 8–59

7

Represent numbers to 1,000

Pages 6–7

The place of each digit in a number tells us its value. Composing and decomposing numbers to 1,000 into hundreds, tens and ones makes them easier to calculate.

We can **compose** and **decompose 3-digit numbers** into **hundreds**, tens and ones and show the **place value** of each **digit**.

To compose a number, we use our knowledge of place value to **create** a number, for example: $300 + 60 + 5 = 365$.

To decompose a number, we use our knowledge of place value to **separate** or **partition** a number, for example: $365 = 300 + 60 + 5$.

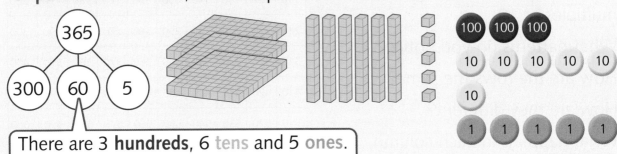

There are 3 **hundreds**, 6 tens and 5 **ones**.
$365 = 3$ **hundreds** $+ 6$ tens $+ 5$ **ones**

To find the **value** of each digit, we look at its position in the place value chart.

The digit 3 is in the **hundreds** position. The value of the 3 is 3 **hundreds** or **300**.

The digit 5 is in the ones position. The value of the 5 is 5 ones or 5.

100s	10s	1s
3	6	5

The digit 6 is in the tens position. The value of the 6 is 6 tens or 60.

To find the whole number, we **add** the values together.
$300 + 60 + 5 = 365$

This Gattegno chart shows the number 365.

100	200	300	400	500	600	700	800	900
10	20	30	40	50	60	70	80	90
1	2	3	4	5	6	7	8	9

We can say:

There are 3 **hundreds**, 6 tens and 5 **ones** in 365.

We can also say:

365 **is equal to** 300 add 60 add 5.

Say Compose a 3-digit number by pointing to numbers in the **hundreds**, tens, and ones rows.

Say your number in different ways.

100	200	300	400	500	600	700	800	900
10	20	30	40	50	60	70	80	90
1	2	3	4	5	6	7	8	9

What numbers have been decomposed to show their place value?

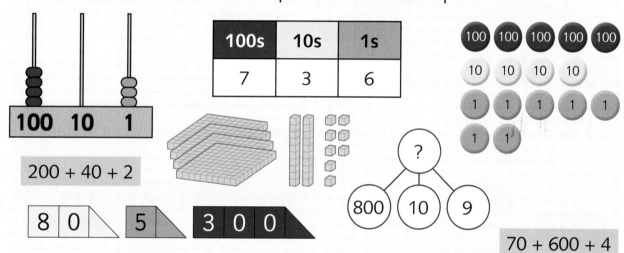

100 10 1

200 + 40 + 2

100s	10s	1s
7	3	6

8 0   5   3 0 0

?
800   10   9

70 + 600 + 4

100 to 999

Choose a 3-digit number.

How many different ways can you decompose your number into **hundreds**, tens and ones?

Build

What objects could you use?

Draw

What pictures or models might you draw?

Say

Which part shows the **hundreds**? Which part shows the tens? Which part shows the ones?

How many **hundreds**, tens and ones are there?

Write

How would you write your number as an addition calculation?

Pages 10-11, 14-19, 22-45, 56-59

9

Represent numbers to 1,000 in different ways

Pages 6-9

We can decompose numbers to 1,000 into hundreds, tens and ones to show the place value of each digit. We can also decompose (or regroup) 3-digit numbers in other ways.

We can **decompose** or **partition** 365 into **hundreds**, tens and ones using our knowledge of the place value position of the digits.

Remember

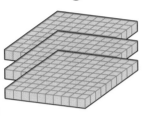 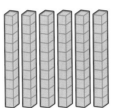 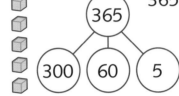

$365 = 300 + 60 + 5$

365

300 · 60 · 5

Numbers can also be decomposed (or **regrouped**) in other ways to help with calculations.

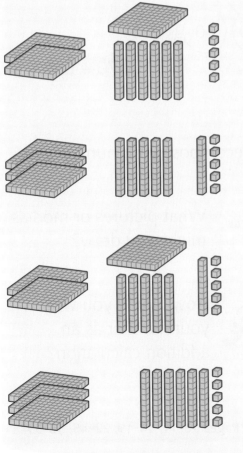

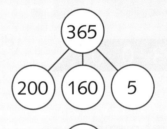

365

200 · 160 · 5

$365 = 200 + 160 + 5$

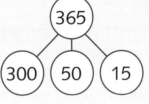

365

300 · 50 · 15

$365 = 300 + 50 + 15$

365

200 · 150 · 15

$365 = 200 + 150 + 15$

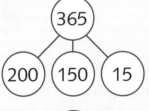

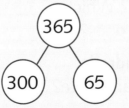

365

300 · 65

$365 = 300 + 65$

How else could you regroup 365?

We can decompose 548 into **hundreds**, tens and ones.

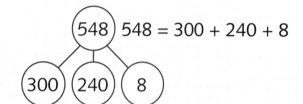

$$548 = 500 + 40 + 8$$

We can regroup 548 in other ways.

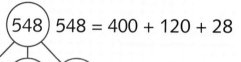

$$548 = 300 + 240 + 8$$

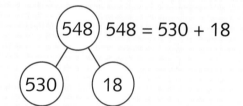

$$548 = 400 + 120 + 28$$

$$548 = 530 + 18$$

Can you think of other ways to regroup 548?

100 to 999

Choose a 3-digit number.

How many different ways can you regroup your number?

What objects could you use?

What pictures or models might you draw?

How would you write your number as an addition calculation?

Pages 22-45, 56-59

Number and place value

Number lines to 1,000

Pages 6-7

We can use number lines to help us identify the previous and next multiple of 10 and 100, and to estimate the position of numbers in the counting sequence. We also read and interpret number lines in the form of a scale on measuring instruments and graphs.

Let's begin by looking at this number line to 100.

These lines are called **interval lines** or just **intervals**.

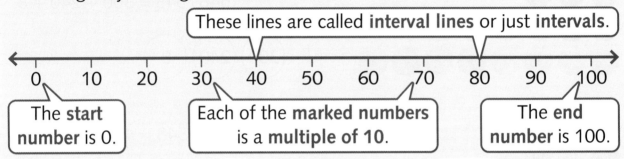

The **start number** is 0.

Each of the **marked numbers** is a **multiple of 10**.

The **end number** is 100.

Look at these number lines. They are divided into 2, 4, 5 and 10 **equal parts**.

This is important because these are the intervals commonly found on measuring instruments and graph scales.

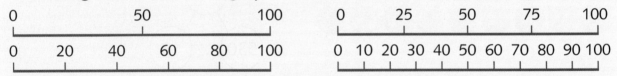

Count on and **back** in **steps of** 50, 25, 20 and 10 from 0 to 100 and beyond.

Now look at this number line.

How is it the same as the number lines above? How is it different?

How is it the same as the number line above?

How is it different?

Each of the marked numbers on this number line is a **multiple of 100**.

What numbers do the **unmarked intervals** stand for?

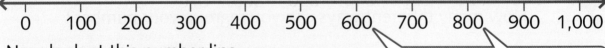

Count on and back in **steps of 100** from 0 to 1,000.

12

Look carefully at the start and end numbers on these number lines.

What numbers are the arrows pointing to?

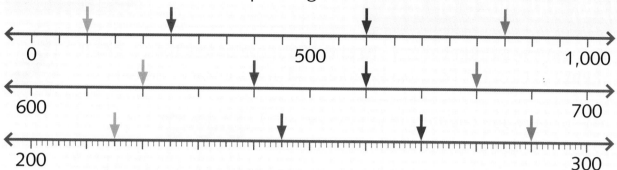

Which multiples of 100 do each of these numbers come before and after?

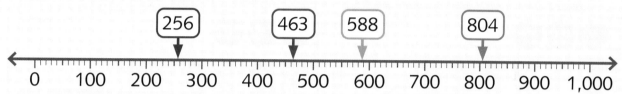

Look carefully at the start and end numbers on these number lines.

The numbers marked below the number lines, such as 410 and 850, are 3-digit multiples of 10.

Which 3-digit multiples of 10 do each of these numbers come before and after?

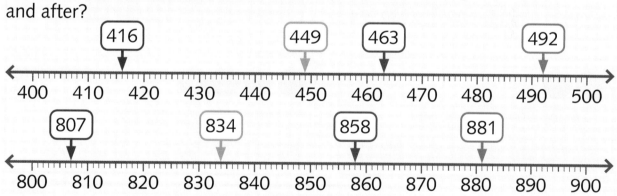

Estimate the number each arrow is pointing to.

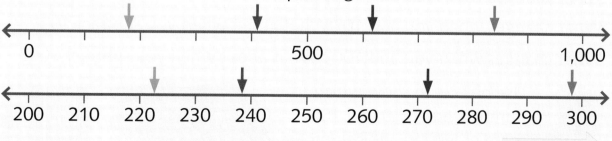

Pages 14-21

1, 10, 100 more or less

Pages 6-9, 12-13

Knowing what number is 1, 10 and 100 more or less than a given number helps us to compare, order, add and subtract numbers.

The place value counters below show 1, 10 and 100 **more** or **less** than the number 368.

What numbers are 1, 10 and 100 more or less than 368?

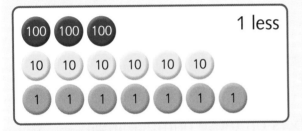

1 less

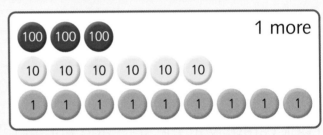

1 more

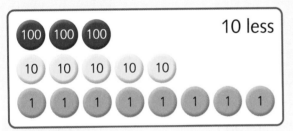

10 less

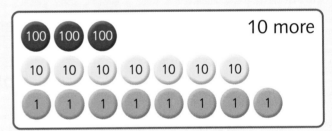

10 more

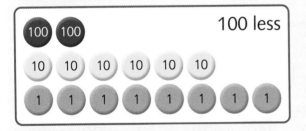

100 less

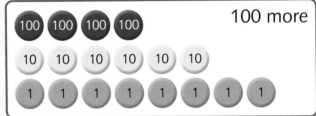

100 more

Look at the place value counters above.

What changes when you **add** 1? What about when you **subtract** 1?

What changes when you add 10? What about when you subtract 10?

What changes when you add 100? What about when you subtract 100?

Use objects to show which numbers are 1, 10 and 100 more or less than this number.

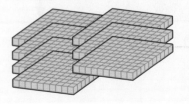

Look at these number cards.

What is 1 more and 1 less than each number?

What is 10 more and 10 less than each number?

What is 100 more and 100 less than each number?

Which numbers were easy to find?

Which were more difficult?

Why was this?

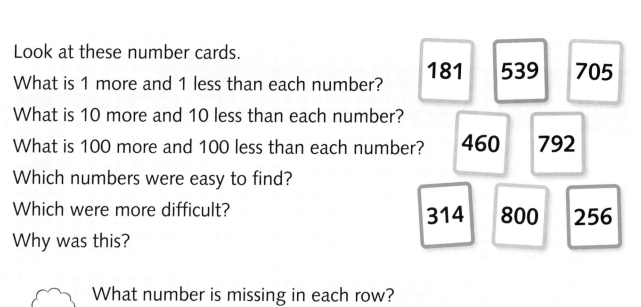

What number is missing in each row?

How did you work out the missing numbers?

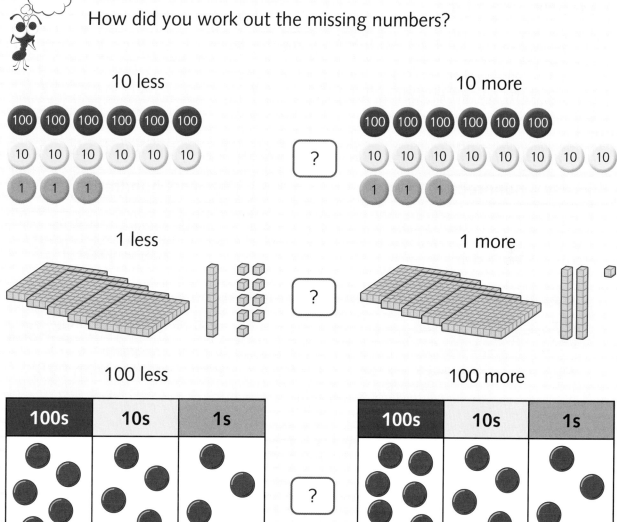

Pages 16-17, 22-45

Compare objects and numbers to 1,000

Pages 6–9, 12–15

We use different words to compare two groups of objects or two numbers. We can also use the symbols >, < and = when we compare numbers.

When **comparing** two groups of **objects**, we can use the words **more**, **fewer** or **the same**.

When comparing two **numbers**, we can use the words **greater than**, **less than** or **equal to**.

We can also use **signs**, or **symbols**, to **compare** two numbers.

It's important to remember what each of these symbols means.

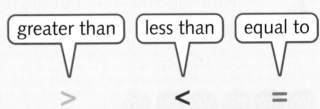

greater than	less than	equal to
>	<	=

When comparing 3-digit numbers, start by looking at the **hundreds** digits.

456 has 4 **hundreds**. ⟩ **456**

456 is greater than 378.

456 > 378

378 has 3 **hundreds**. ⟩ **378**

378 is less than 456.

378 < 456

If the **hundreds** digits are the same, then look at the tens digits.

925 has 2 tens. ⟩ **925**

925 is less than 941.

925 < 941

941 has 4 tens. ⟩ **941**

941 is greater than 925.

941 > 925

If the **hundreds** and tens digits are the same, then look at the ones digits.

253 has 3 ones. ⟩ **253**

253 is less than 257.

253 < 257

257 has 7 ones. ⟩ **257**

257 is greater than 253.

257 > 253

Which is the greater number in each pair?

Should you start by comparing the **hundreds**, tens or ones first? Why?

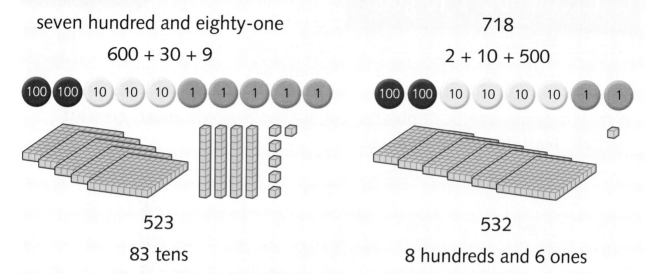

seven hundred and eighty-one

600 + 30 + 9

523

83 tens

718

2 + 10 + 500

532

8 hundreds and 6 ones

Write

Write each pair of numbers above as 3-digit numbers.

Use the greater than or less than symbol to compare each pair of numbers.

We can also use a number line to help compare numbers.

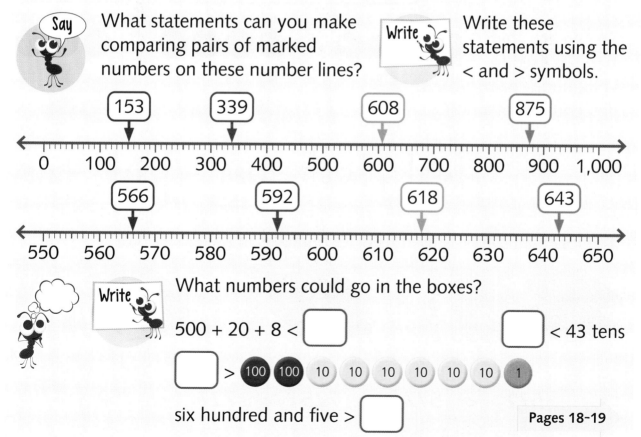

Say

What statements can you make comparing pairs of marked numbers on these number lines?

Write

Write these statements using the < and > symbols.

What numbers could go in the boxes?

500 + 20 + 8 < ☐

☐ < 43 tens

☐ > 100 100 10 10 10 10 10 10 1

six hundred and five > ☐

Pages 18-19

Order numbers to 1,000

Pages 6-9, 12-17

We use different words to order groups of objects or a set of numbers. We can also order numbers using the symbols > and <.

When ordering groups of **objects**, we use these words: **most**, **greatest**, **largest**, **least**, **fewest** or **smallest**.

When ordering a set of **numbers**, we use these words: greatest, largest or smallest.

We can **order** groups of objects or a set of numbers:
 in **ascending** order – from smallest to largest
 or in **descending** order – from largest to smallest.

We can use the symbols > or < to order objects or numbers.

Remember | greater than | less than | equal to
> | < | =

The greater than sign > is used to write numbers in descending order.

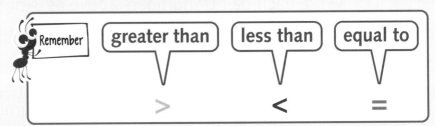

482 > 428 > 288 > 284 > 248

The less than sign < is used to write numbers in ascending order.

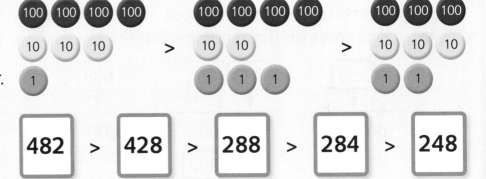

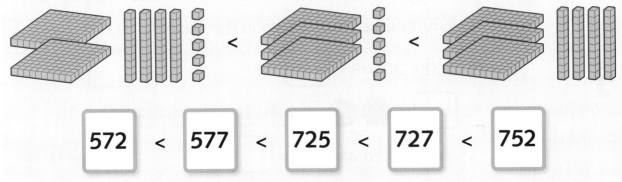

572 < 577 < 725 < 727 < 752

Look at this set of numbers.

What is the same about the numbers?

What's different?

| 601 | 106 | 362 | 160 | 326 |

Which **digits** are the most important ones to consider when ordering a set of 3-digit numbers? Why is this?

When ordering 3-digit numbers, if the **hundreds** digits are equal in **value**, what do you look at next?

Write — Write the set of numbers above in ascending order.

☐ < ☐ < ☐ < ☐ < ☐

Now write the numbers in descending order.

☐ > ☐ > ☐ > ☐ > ☐

What do you notice? Why is this?

We can use a number line to help order numbers.

| 324 | 432 | 243 | 342 | 423 |

243   324 342   423 432

240 260 280 300 320 340 360 380 400 420 440

Write — Use the 500 to 600 number line to order each set of numbers. Start with the smallest number.

☐ < ☐ < ☐ < ☐ < ☐

500 510 520 530 540 550 560 570 580 590 600

| 552 | 502 | 520 | 525 | 505 | | 571 | 517 | 575 | 555 | 515 |

Count in 4s, 8s, 50s and 100s

Pages 6-7, 12-17

Counting in steps – step counting – involves recognising and continuing number patterns. We can use known multiplication facts and the relationship between them to help count in steps.

Counting in steps of 2 and 4

When we **count in steps**, we often see **patterns**.

What do you notice about counting in steps of 2 and in steps of 4?

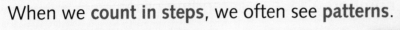

2 4 6 8 10 12 14 16 18 20   4 8 12 16 20

Counting from 0 in 2s gives the **multiples of 2** in the 2 multiplication table.

Counting from 0 in 4s gives the **multiples of 4** in the 4 multiplication table.

What do you notice about the numbers on this number line?

```
0    4    8    12   16   20   24   28   32   36   40
```

Say
- **Count on** in 4s from 0 to 40.
- **Count back** in 4s from 40 to 0.
- Starting from a number other than 0, count on in steps of 4 to 40.
- Starting from a number other than 40, count back in steps of 4 to 0.

Counting in steps of 8

What do you notice about the numbers on this number line?

Counting from 0 in 8s gives the **multiples of 8** in the 8 multiplication table.

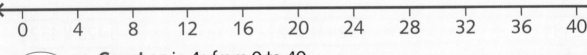

```
0    8    16   24   32   40   48   56   64   72   80
```

Look at the two number lines above.

Can you spot any patterns in the multiples of 4 and the multiples of 8?

Counting in steps of 50

Look at the two number lines below.

How are they the same? How are they different? What patterns do you notice?

What is the connection between the **multiples of 5** and the **multiples of 50**?

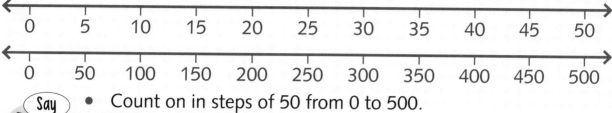

| 0 | 5 | 10 | 15 | 20 | 25 | 30 | 35 | 40 | 45 | 50 |

| 0 | 50 | 100 | 150 | 200 | 250 | 300 | 350 | 400 | 450 | 500 |

Say
- Count on in steps of 50 from 0 to 500.
- Count back in steps of 50 from 500 to 0.
- Choose numbers other than 0 and 500 and count on and back in steps of 50.

Counting in steps of 100

Look at this number grid. It shows the 2-digit and 3-digit multiples of 10.

What patterns do you notice?

Say
- Choose a number on the grid and count on in steps of 100.
- Choose a number on the grid and count back in steps of 100.

10	20	30	40	50	60	70	80	90	100
110	120	130	140	150	160	170	180	190	200
210	220	230	240	250	260	270	280	290	300
310	320	330	340	350	360	370	380	390	400
410	420	430	440	450	460	470	480	490	500
510	520	530	540	550	560	570	580	590	600
610	620	630	640	650	660	670	680	690	700
710	720	730	740	750	760	770	780	790	800
810	820	830	840	850	860	870	880	890	900
910	920	930	940	950	960	970	980	990	1,000

Use the grid to count on and back in steps of 10.

This number line shows the **multiples of 100** from 0 to 1,000.

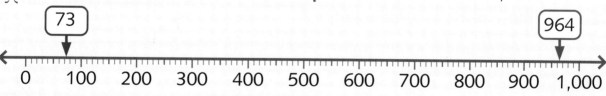

73   964

| 0 | 100 | 200 | 300 | 400 | 500 | 600 | 700 | 800 | 900 | 1,000 |

Say
- Starting at 73, count on in steps of 100.
- Starting at 964, count back in steps of 100.
- Say any 2-digit number, such as 41. Count on from it in steps of 100.
- Say a 3-digit number with 9 **hundreds**, such as 985. Count back from it in steps of 100.

Pages 34-35, 50-53

Addition and subtraction facts to 20

Pages 6-11, 14-15

Being able to recall the addition and subtraction facts to 10 and 20 instantly is important for adding and subtracting 2-digit and 3-digit numbers.

This ten frame and part-whole model show the same addition and subtraction facts.

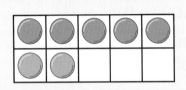

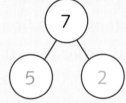

These are a fact family for 7.

5 + 2 = 7	7 − 2 = 5
2 + 5 = 7	7 − 5 = 2

Addition and subtraction are related – they are inverse operations.

That means they are opposite operations – addition reverses subtraction, and subtraction reverses addition.

We can use the inverse relationship between addition and subtraction to help find related facts.

A 'fact family' is a set of related addition and subtraction number sentences that include the same numbers. If we know one fact then we can use this to recall other related facts.

Addition is commutative – it can be done in any order.

So, 5 + 2 = 7 and 2 + 5 = 7

Addition and subtraction are related.

So, if you know that 5 + 2 = 7 you also know that 7 − 2 = 5 and that 7 − 5 = 2

Look at these other fact families for 7.

Say What addition and subtraction number sentences can you say for each family fact?

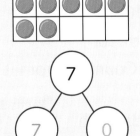

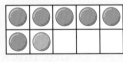

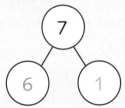

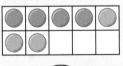

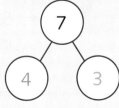

When working out the answer to an unknown fact, it's important to look carefully at the numbers and decide on the most effective and efficient mental strategy.

We can use known addition and subtraction facts to 10 to help recall facts to 20.

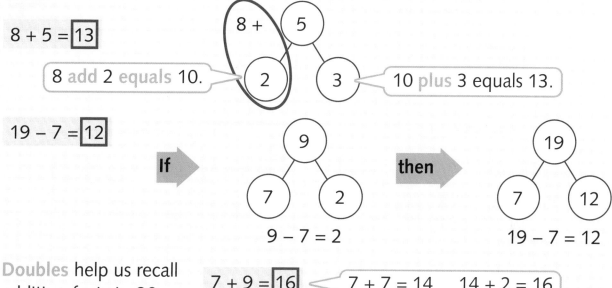

$8 + 5 = \boxed{13}$

8 add 2 equals 10.

10 plus 3 equals 13.

$19 - 7 = \boxed{12}$

If

$9 - 7 = 2$

then

$19 - 7 = 12$

Doubles help us recall addition facts to 20.

$7 + 9 = \boxed{16}$ $7 + 7 = 14$ $14 + 2 = 16$

Addition can be done in any order – it's commutative.

Putting the larger number first and counting on makes addition easier.

Remember

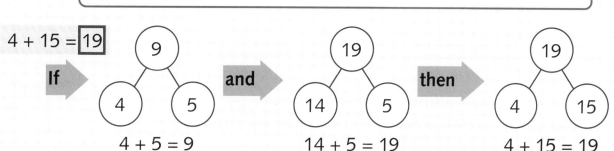

$4 + 15 = \boxed{19}$

If

$4 + 5 = 9$

and

$14 + 5 = 19$

then

$4 + 15 = 19$

We can think of subtraction as finding the difference, which means comparing the numbers and counting on or counting back.

Would you count on or count back? Why?

$15 - 12 = \boxed{3}$

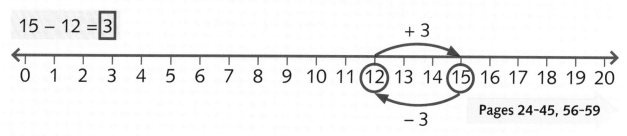

+ 3

– 3

Pages 24-45, 56-59

Related addition and subtraction facts

Pages 6-11, 14-15, 22-23

Being able to recall the addition and subtraction facts to 20 helps us to add and subtract multiples of 10.

$80 + 70 = \boxed{150}$ ← We can use the known fact $8 + 7 = 15$ to help.

Change the ones to tens.

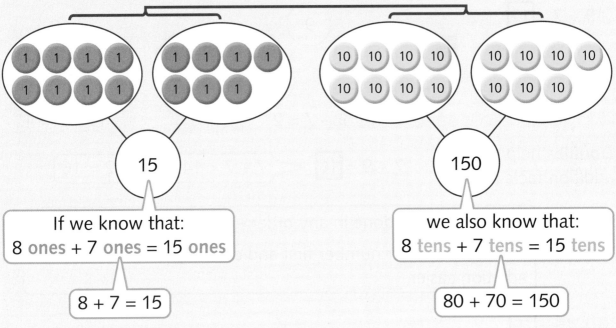

15

150

If we know that:
8 ones + 7 ones = 15 ones

we also know that:
8 tens + 7 tens = 15 tens

$8 + 7 = 15$

$80 + 70 = 150$

- Addition can be done in any order – it's commutative.
- Fact families – addition and subtraction are related. If we know one addition or subtraction fact then we know three other related facts.

Remember

So,

$8 + 7 = 15$
$7 + 8 = 15$
$15 - 7 = 8$
$15 - 8 = 7$

and

$80 + 70 = 150$
$70 + 80 = 150$
$150 - 70 = 80$
$150 - 80 = 70$

$140 - 60 = \boxed{80}$ — We can use the known fact $14 - 6 = 8$.

Change the ones to tens.

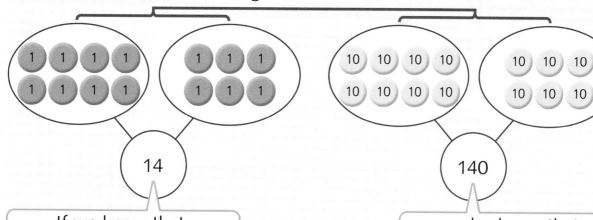

If we know that:
14 ones – 6 ones = 8 ones — $14 - 6 = 8$

we also know that:
14 tens – 6 tens = 8 tens

 Say If you know that $140 - 60 = 80$, what other addition and subtraction facts do you know?

$140 - 60 = 80$

Say What numbers are missing from these part-whole models and calculations?

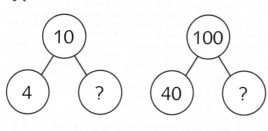

$4 + \boxed{} = 10$

$\boxed{} + 4 = 10$

$10 - \boxed{} = 4$

$10 - 4 = \boxed{}$

$40 + \boxed{} = 100$

$\boxed{} + 40 = 100$

$100 - \boxed{} = 40$

$100 - 40 = \boxed{}$

 Build **Draw** Use objects or draw a model to show the answers to these calculations.

$90 + 40 = \boxed{}$

$160 - 90 = \boxed{}$

 Write If you know each of these answers, what other related facts do you know?

Pages 30–45

Add a 3-digit number and 1s

Pages 6-11, 14-15, 22-23

We can use partitioning and known addition facts to add a 1-digit number to a 3-digit number, such as 264 + 5 or 358 + 6.

Each part of an addition calculation has a special name. It's helpful to know these names.

We can decompose (or partition) 264 into **hundreds, tens** and **ones** and add the **ones**.

addend   addend

$$264 + 5 = \boxed{269}$$

sum or total

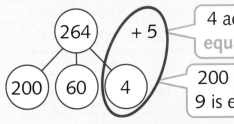

4 add 5 is equal to 9.

200 plus 60 plus 9 is equal to 269.

$$264 + 5 = 200 + 60 + 4 + 5$$
$$= 200 + 60 + 9$$
$$= 269$$

We can decompose (or regroup) 264 in different ways.

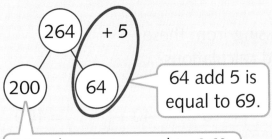

64 add 5 is equal to 69.

200 plus 69 is equal to 269.

$$264 + 5 = 200 + 64 + 5$$
$$= 200 + 69$$
$$= 269$$

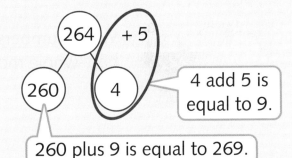

4 add 5 is equal to 9.

260 plus 9 is equal to 269.

$$264 + 5 = 260 + 4 + 5$$
$$= 260 + 9$$
$$= 269$$

$$358 + 6 = \boxed{364}$$

We can decompose 358 into **hundreds, tens** and **ones** and add the **ones**.

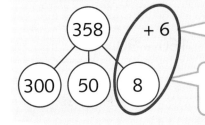

8 add 6 is equal to 14.

300 plus 50 plus 14 is equal to 364.

$$358 + 6 = 300 + 50 + 8 + 6$$
$$= 300 + 50 + 14$$
$$= 364$$

We can regroup 358 in different ways.

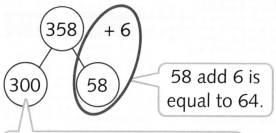

58 add 6 is equal to 64.

300 plus 64 is equal to 364.

$$358 + 6 = 300 + 58 + 6$$
$$= 300 + 64$$
$$= 364$$

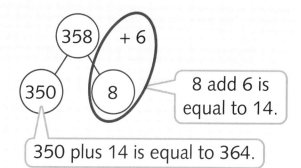

8 add 6 is equal to 14.

350 plus 14 is equal to 364.

$$358 + 6 = 350 + 8 + 6$$
$$= 350 + 14$$
$$= 364$$

We can work this out using a number line.

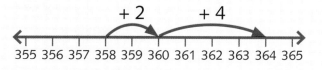

or

We can also use place value counters.

First partition 358 into **hundreds**, tens and ones.

Then add the ones. As there are more than 10 ones we need to regroup 10 ones into 1 ten.

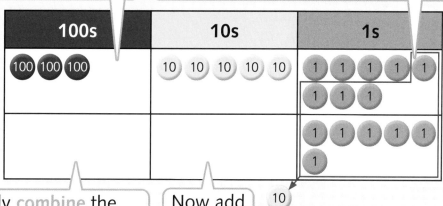

100s	10s	1s

Finally combine the ones, tens and **hundreds**.

Now add the tens.

Look at this calculation: 842 + 9 = 851

We can work this out by adding 10 and subtracting 1.

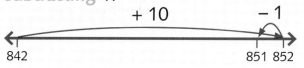

$$842 + 9 = 842 + 10 - 1$$
$$= 852 - 1$$
$$= 851$$

Pages 30-31, 34-35, 38-39, 42-43

Subtract a 3-digit number and Is

Pages 6-11, 14-15, 22-23

We can use partitioning and known subtraction facts to subtract a 1-digit number from a 3-digit number, such as $328 - 5$ or $275 - 8$.

Each part of a **subtraction calculation** has a special name. It's helpful to know these names.

We can **decompose** (or **partition**) 328 into **hundreds**, **tens** and **ones** and **subtract** the **ones**.

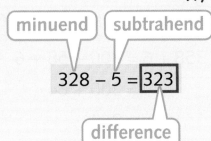

$$328 - 5 = \boxed{323}$$

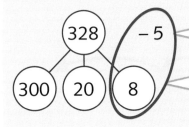

8 subtract 5 is equal to 3.

300 plus 20 plus 3 is equal to 323.

$328 - 5 = 300 + 20 + 8 - 5$

$= 300 + 20 + 3$

$= 323$

We can decompose (or **regroup**) 328 in different ways, for example:

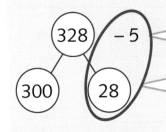

28 subtract 5 is equal to 23.

300 plus 23 is equal to 323.

$328 - 5 = 300 + 28 - 5$

$= 300 + 23$

$= 323$

$275 - 8 = \boxed{267}$ We can regroup 275 into $200 + 75$ and subtract the **ones**.

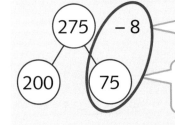

75 subtract 8 is equal to 67.

200 plus 67 is equal to 267.

$275 - 8 = 200 + 75 - 8$

$= 200 + 67$

$= 267$

We can regroup 275 in different ways, for example:

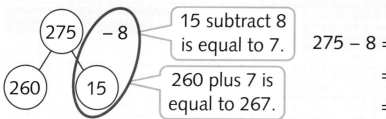

$$275 - 8 = 260 + 15 - 8$$
$$= 260 + 7$$
$$= 267$$

15 subtract 8 is equal to 7.

260 plus 7 is equal to 267.

We can work this out using a number line.

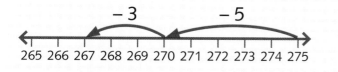 or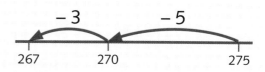

We can also use place value counters.

First partition 275 into **hundreds**, tens and ones.

Then subtract the ones. There are 5 ones in 275. But we need to subtract 8 ones. As there aren't enough ones in 275 we need to exchange 1 ten for 10 ones.

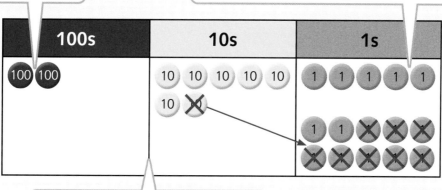

100s	10s	1s
100 100	10 10 10 10 10 / 10 ⊗	1 1 1 1 1 / 1 1 ⊗ ⊗ ⊗ / ⊗ ⊗ ⊗ ⊗ ⊗

Finally place the partitioned number back together.

Look at this calculation: 563 − 9 = 554

We can work this out by subtracting 10 and adding 1.

$$563 - 9 = 563 - 10 + 1$$
$$= 553 + 1$$
$$= 554$$

+ 1   − 10

553 554   563

Pages 32-35, 40-41, 44-45

Add a 3-digit number and 10s

Pages 6–11, 14–15, 22–27

We can use partitioning and known addition facts to add a multiple of 10 to a 3-digit number, such as 237 + 40 or 578 + 50.

$237 + 40 = \boxed{277}$

We can **decompose** (or **partition**) 237 into **hundreds**, **tens** and **ones** and **add** the **tens**.

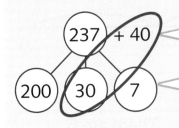

30 add 40 is equal to 70.

200 plus 70 plus 7 is equal to 277.

$$237 + 40 = 200 + 30 + 7 + 40$$
$$= 200 + 70 + 7$$
$$= 277$$

We can decompose (or **regroup**) 237 in different ways.

Addition can be done in any order – it's **commutative**.

Remember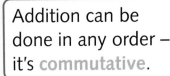

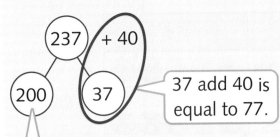

37 add 40 is equal to 77.

200 plus 77 is equal to 277.

$$237 + 40 = 200 + 37 + 40$$
$$= 200 + 77$$
$$= 277$$

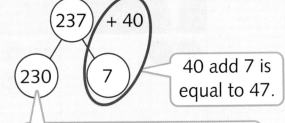

40 add 7 is equal to 47.

230 plus 47 is equal to 277.

$$237 + 40 = 230 + 7 + 40$$
$$= 230 + 47$$
$$= 277$$

$578 + 50 = \boxed{628}$

We can decompose 578 into **hundreds**, **tens** and **ones** and add the **tens**.

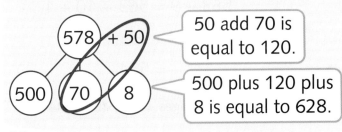

50 add 70 is equal to 120.

500 plus 120 plus 8 is equal to 628.

$$578 + 50 = 500 + 70 + 8 + 50$$
$$= 500 + 120 + 8$$
$$= 628$$

We can regroup 578 in different ways.

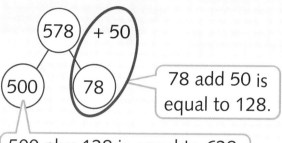

78 add 50 is equal to 128.

500 plus 128 is equal to 628.

$578 + 50 = 500 + 78 + 50$
$= 500 + 128$
$= 628$

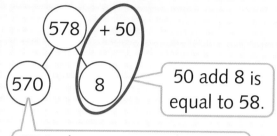

50 add 8 is equal to 58.

570 plus 58 is equal to 628.

$578 + 50 = 570 + 8 + 50$
$= 570 + 58$
$= 628$

We can work this out using a number line.

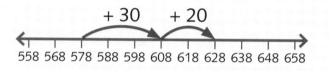

or

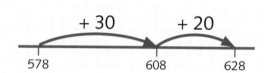

We can also use place value counters.

First partition 578 into **hundreds**, tens and ones.

Then add the tens. As there are more than 10 tens we need to regroup 10 tens into 1 **hundred**.

Finally combine the ones, tens and **hundreds**.

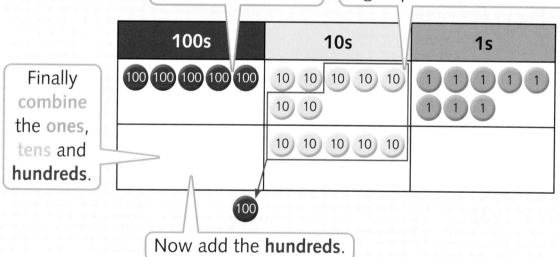

Now add the **hundreds**.

Use your preferred method to work out the answers to these calculations.

$481 + 39 =$ ☐

$658 + 61 =$ ☐

Pages 34-35, 38-39, 42-43

Pages 6–11, 14–15, 22–25, 28–29

Subtract a 3-digit number and 10s

We can use partitioning and known subtraction facts to subtract a multiple of 10 from a 3-digit number, such as 486 − 30 or 739 − 60.

486 − 30 = 456

We can **decompose** (or **partition**) 486 into **hundreds**, **tens** and **ones** and **subtract** the **tens**.

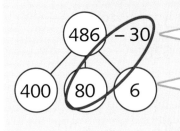

80 subtract 30 **is equal to** 50.

400 **plus** 50 plus 6 is equal to 456.

$$486 - 30 = 400 + 80 + 6 - 30$$
$$= 400 + 50 + 6$$
$$= 456$$

We can decompose (or **regroup**) 486 in different ways, for example:

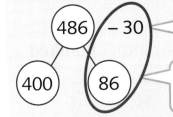

86 subtract 30 is equal to 56.

400 plus 56 is equal to 456.

$$486 - 30 = 400 + 86 - 30$$
$$= 400 + 56$$
$$= 456$$

739 − 60 = 679

We can regroup 739 into 600 + 139 and subtract the **tens**.

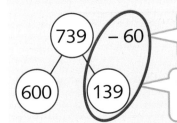

139 subtract 60 is equal to 79.

600 plus 79 is equal to 679.

$$739 - 60 = 600 + 139 - 60$$
$$= 600 + 79$$
$$= 679$$

We can regroup 739 in different ways, for example:

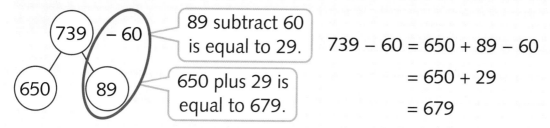

89 subtract 60 is equal to 29.

650 plus 29 is equal to 679.

$739 - 60 = 650 + 89 - 60$
$= 650 + 29$
$= 679$

We can work this out using a number line.

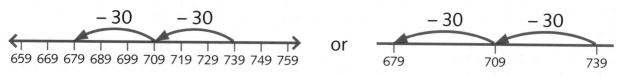

or

We can also use place value counters.

First partition 739 into **hundreds**, tens and ones.

Then subtract the tens. There are 3 tens in 739. But we need to subtract 6 tens. As there aren't enough tens in 739, we need to exchange 1 **hundred** for 10 tens.

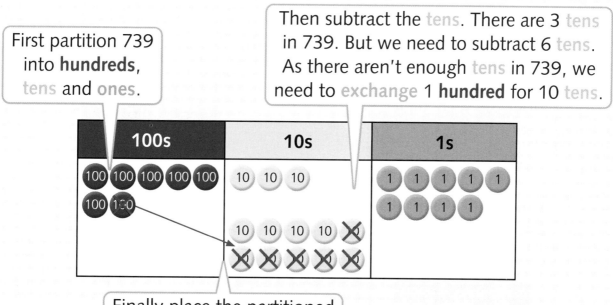

Finally place the partitioned number back together.

Use your preferred method to work out the answers to these calculations.

$321 - 59 =$ ☐ $423 - 61 =$ ☐

Pages 34-35, 40-41, 44-45

Add and subtract a 3-digit number and 100s

Pages 6-11, 14-15, 20-33

We can use our understanding of place value and known addition and subtraction facts to add and subtract a multiple of 100 to or from a 3-digit number, such as $475 + 500$ or $658 - 300$.

$475 + 500 = \boxed{975}$

We can **decompose** (or **partition**) 475 into **hundreds**, **tens** and **ones** and **add** the **hundreds**.

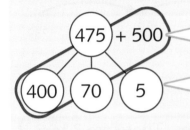

400 add 500 is equal to 900.

900 plus 70 plus 5 is equal to 975.

$$475 + 500 = 400 + 70 + 5 + 500$$
$$= 900 + 70 + 5$$
$$= 975$$

What do you notice about the **hundreds** digits?

What about the tens digit?

What about the **ones** digit?

What changes when we add a **hundreds** number?

What stays the same?

We can represent the calculation with place value counters.

First partition 475 into **hundreds**, tens and **ones**.

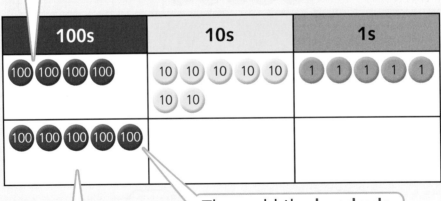

Then add the **hundreds**.

Finally combine the ones, tens and **hundreds**.

34

$658 - 300 = \boxed{358}$

We can decompose 658 into **hundreds**, tens and **ones** and subtract the **hundreds**.

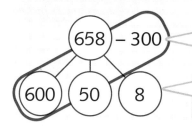

600 subtract 300 is equal to 300.

300 plus 50 plus 8 is equal to 358.

$658 - 300 = 600 + 50 + 8 - 300$

$= 300 + 50 + 8$

$= 358$

What do you notice about the **hundreds** digits?

What about the tens digit?

What about the ones digit?

What changes when we subtract a **hundreds** number?

What stays the same?

We can represent the calculation with place value counters.

First partition 658 into **hundreds**, tens and **ones**.

100s	10s	1s
100 100 100 100 100 100	10 10 10 10 10	1 1 1 1 1 1 1 1

Then subtract the **hundreds**.

Finally place the partitioned number back together.

Use your preferred method to work out the answers to these calculations.

$261 + 301 = \boxed{}$ $718 - 201 = \boxed{}$

$597 + 299 = \boxed{}$ $919 - 499 = \boxed{}$

Pages 38-45

35

Add and subtract two 2-digit numbers

Pages 6-11, 14-15, 22-25

To add and subtract two 2-digit numbers, such as 86 + 67 or 83 − 45, we need to partition 2-digit numbers into tens and ones and have instant recall of the addition and subtraction facts to 20.

$34 + 83 = \boxed{117}$

First partition both numbers into tens and ones.

⚠ **ALWAYS:**
Estimate
Calculate
Check

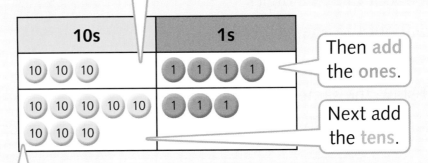

Then add the ones.

Next add the tens.

Finally combine the ones and tens.

What do you notice about the sum of the tens? What do you need to do?

We can record this in columns.

```
    3 4
  + 8 3
        7      leads to        3 4
  1 1 0                      + 8 3
  1 1 7                      1 1 7
```

$86 + 67 = \boxed{153}$

First partition both numbers into tens and ones.

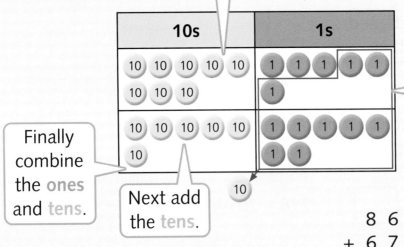

Then add the ones. As there are more than 10 ones, we need to regroup 10 ones into 1 ten.

Finally combine the ones and tens.

Next add the tens.

What do you notice about the sum of the tens? What do you need to do?

We can record this in columns.

```
    8 6
  + 6 7
      1 3      leads to        8 6
  1 4 0                      + 6 7
  1 5 3                      1 5 3
                                1
```

$67 - 35 = \boxed{32}$

First partition 67 into tens and ones.

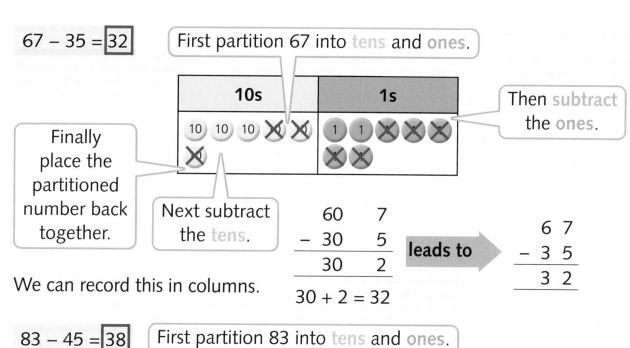

Then subtract the ones.

Finally place the partitioned number back together.

Next subtract the tens.

We can record this in columns.

$$
\begin{array}{rr}
60 & 7 \\
- \ 30 & 5 \\
\hline
30 & 2
\end{array}
$$

$30 + 2 = 32$

leads to

$$
\begin{array}{r}
6 \ 7 \\
- \ 3 \ 5 \\
\hline
3 \ 2
\end{array}
$$

$83 - 45 = \boxed{38}$

First partition 83 into tens and ones.

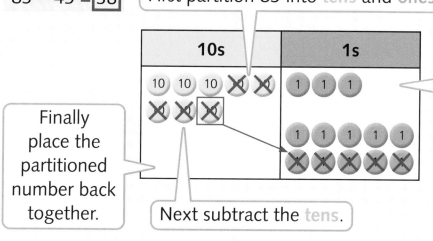

Then subtract the ones. There are 3 ones in 83. But we need to subtract 5 ones. As there aren't enough ones in 83, we need to exchange 1 ten for 10 ones.

Finally place the partitioned number back together.

Next subtract the tens.

We can record this in columns.

$$
\begin{array}{rr}
^{70} & ^{13} \\
\cancel{80} & \cancel{3} \\
- \ 40 & 5 \\
\hline
30 & 8
\end{array}
$$

$30 + 8 = 38$

leads to

$$
\begin{array}{r}
^7 \ ^1 \\
\cancel{8} \ 3 \\
- \ 4 \ 5 \\
\hline
3 \ 8
\end{array}
$$

You can also write the exchanged values like this.

$$
\begin{array}{r}
^7 \ ^{13} \\
\cancel{8} \ \cancel{3} \\
- \ 4 \ 5 \\
\hline
3 \ 8
\end{array}
$$

It's also important to know complements to 100 – pairs of numbers that total 100.

The ones digits total 1 ten, so we need 9 more tens to make a total of 100.

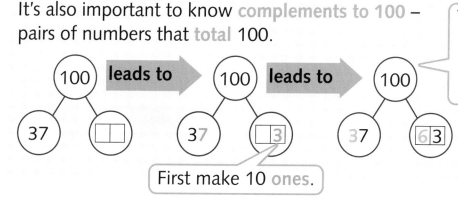

First make 10 ones.

Pages 38-45

Add 2-digit and 3-digit numbers

Pages 6-11, 14-15, 22-27, 30-31, 34-37

To add 2-digit and 3-digit numbers, such as 423 + 35 or 357 + 84, we need to line up the digits carefully in place value columns.

423 + 35 = 458

⚠ **ALWAYS:**
Estimate
Calculate
Check

First partition both numbers into **hundreds**, tens and ones.

Then add the ones.

100s	10s	1s
100 100 100 100	10 10	1 1 1
	10 10 10	1 1 1 1 1

Finally combine the ones, tens and **hundreds**.

Next add the tens.

```
    4 2 3
  +   3 5
        8
      5 0
    4 0 0
    4 5 8
```

We can record this in columns.

leads to

```
    4 2 3
  +   3 5
    4 5 8
```

236 + 48 = 284

First partition both numbers into **hundreds**, tens and ones.

Then add the ones. As there are more than 10 ones, we need to regroup 10 ones into 1 ten.

100s	10s	1s
100 100	10 10 10	1 1 1 1 1 / 1
	10 10 10 10	1 1 1 1 1 / 1 1 1

Finally combine the ones, tens and **hundreds**.

Next add the tens.

We can record this in columns.

```
    2 3 6
  +   4 8
      1 4
      7 0
    2 0 0
    2 8 4
```

leads to

```
    2 3 6
  +   4 8
    2 8 4
      1
```

38

$572 + 53 = \boxed{625}$

First partition both numbers into **hundreds**, tens and ones.

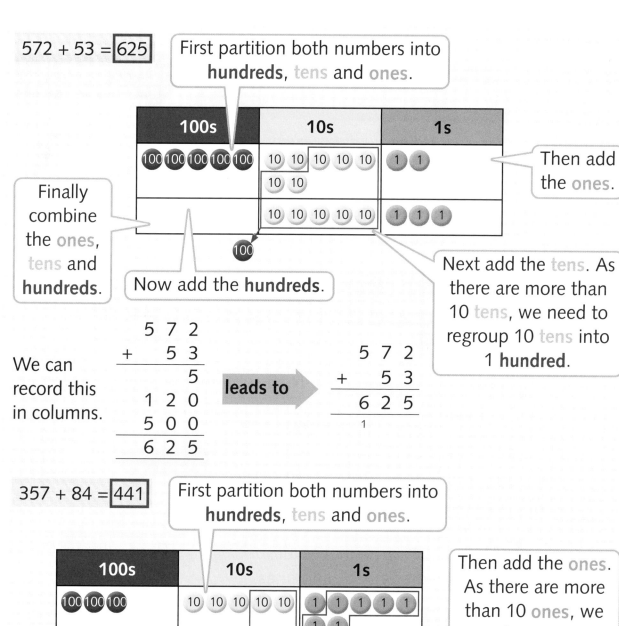

100s	10s	1s
100 100 100 100 100	10 10 10 10 10 10 10	1 1
	10 10 10 10 10	1 1 1
100		

Then add the ones.

Next add the tens. As there are more than 10 tens, we need to regroup 10 tens into 1 **hundred**.

Finally combine the ones, tens and **hundreds**.

Now add the **hundreds**.

We can record this in columns.

```
    5 7 2
  +   5 3
  ───────
        5
    1 2 0
    5 0 0
  ───────
    6 2 5
```

leads to

```
    5 7 2
  +   5 3
  ───────
    6 2 5
      1
```

$357 + 84 = \boxed{441}$

First partition both numbers into **hundreds**, tens and ones.

100s	10s	1s
100 100 100	10 10 10 10 10	1 1 1 1 1 1 1
	10 10 10 10 10 10 10 10	1 1 1 1
100	10	

Then add the ones. As there are more than 10 ones, we need to regroup 10 ones into 1 ten.

Next add the tens. As there are more than 10 tens, we need to regroup 10 tens into 1 **hundred**.

Finally combine the ones, tens and **hundreds**.

Now add the **hundreds**.

We can record this in columns.

```
    3 5 7
  +   8 4
  ───────
      1 1
    1 3 0
    3 0 0
  ───────
    4 4 1
```

leads to

```
    3 5 7
  +   8 4
  ───────
    4 4 1
    1 1
```

Pages 42-43

Addition and subtraction

Subtract 2-digit and 3-digit numbers

Pages 6-11, 14-15, 22-25, 28-29, 32-37

To subtract 2-digit and 3-digit numbers, such as 769 – 32 or 675 – 88, we need to line up the digits carefully in place value columns.

769 – 32 = 737

⚠ **ALWAYS:**
Estimate
Calculate
Check

First **partition** 769 into **hundreds**, tens and ones.

Then subtract the ones.

100s	10s	1s

Next subtract the tens.

Finally place the partitioned number back together.

We can record this in columns.

	700	60	9
–		30	2
	700	30	7

700 + 30 + 7 = 737

leads to

```
  7 6 9
–   3 2
  7 3 7
```

374 – 56 = 318

First partition 374 into **hundreds**, tens and ones.

Then subtract the ones. There are 4 ones in 374, and we need to subtract 6 ones. As there aren't enough ones in 374, exchange 1 ten for 10 ones.

100s	10s	1s

Finally place the partitioned number back together.

Next subtract the tens.

You can also write the exchanged values like this.

We can record this in columns.

	300	60 / 7̶0̶	14 / 4̶
–		50	6
	300	10	8

300 + 10 + 8 = 318

leads to

```
      6  1
  3 7̶ 4
–   5  6
  3 1  8
```

```
      6  14
  3 7̶ 4̶
–    5  6
  3  1  8
```

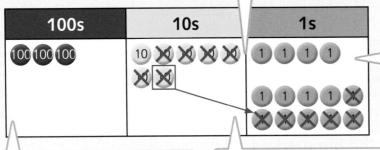

$527 - 62 = \boxed{465}$

First partition 527 into **hundreds**, tens and ones.

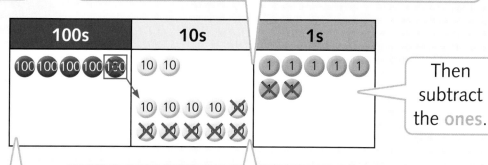

100s	10s	1s

Then subtract the ones.

Next subtract the tens. There are 2 tens in 527, and we need to subtract 6 tens. As there aren't enough tens in 527, exchange 1 **hundred** for 10 tens.

Finally place the partitioned number back together.

We can record this in columns.

$$
\begin{array}{ccc}
\overset{400}{\cancel{500}} & \overset{120}{\cancel{20}} & 7 \\
- & 60 & 2 \\
\hline
400 & 60 & 5 \\
\end{array}
$$

$400 + 60 + 5 = 465$

leads to

You can also write the exchanged values like this.

$$
\begin{array}{ccc}
^4 & ^1 & \\
\cancel{5} & 2 & 7 \\
- & 6 & 2 \\
\hline
4 & 6 & 5 \\
\end{array}
\qquad
\begin{array}{ccc}
^4 & ^{12} & \\
\cancel{5} & \cancel{2} & 7 \\
- & 6 & 2 \\
\hline
4 & 6 & 5 \\
\end{array}
$$

$675 - 88 = \boxed{587}$

First partition 675 into **hundreds**, tens and ones.

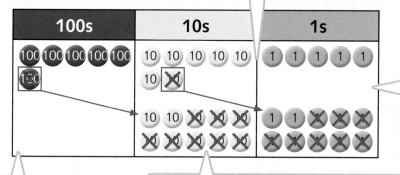

100s	10s	1s

Then subtract the ones. There are 5 ones in 675, and we need to subtract 8 ones. As there aren't enough ones in 675, exchange 1 ten for 10 ones.

Finally place the partitioned number back together.

Next subtract the tens. There are 7 tens in 675, and we need to subtract 8 tens. As there aren't enough tens in 675, exchange 1 **hundred** for 10 tens.

We can record this in columns.

$$
\begin{array}{ccc}
\overset{500}{\cancel{600}} & \overset{160}{\cancel{70}} & \overset{15}{\cancel{5}} \\
- & 80 & 8 \\
\hline
500 & 80 & 7 \\
\end{array}
$$

$500 + 80 + 7 = 587$

leads to

You can also write the exchanged values like this.

$$
\begin{array}{ccc}
^5 & ^{16} & ^1 \\
\cancel{6} & \cancel{7} & 5 \\
- & 8 & 8 \\
\hline
5 & 8 & 7 \\
\end{array}
\qquad
\begin{array}{ccc}
^5 & ^{16} & ^{15} \\
\cancel{6} & \cancel{7} & \cancel{5} \\
- & 8 & 8 \\
\hline
5 & 8 & 7 \\
\end{array}
$$

Pages 44-45

Add two 3-digit numbers

Pages 6-11, 14-15, 22-27, 30-31, 34-39

To add two 3-digit numbers, such as 264 + 132 or 387 + 456, we need to partition the numbers into hundreds, tens and ones and have instant recall of the addition facts to 20.

264 + 132 = 396

⚠ **ALWAYS:**
Estimate
Calculate
Check

Finally combine the ones, tens and hundreds.

Now add the hundreds.

First partition both numbers into hundreds, tens and ones.

Then add the ones.

Next add the tens.

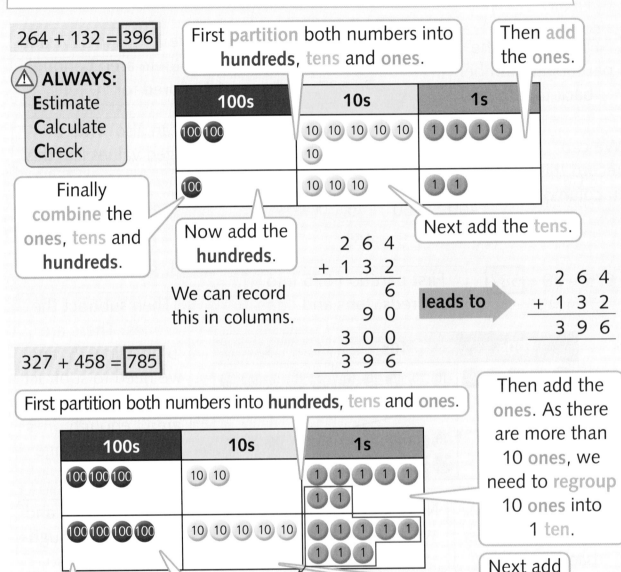

We can record this in columns.

```
  2 6 4
+ 1 3 2
      6
    9 0
  3 0 0
  3 9 6
```

leads to

```
  2 6 4
+ 1 3 2
  3 9 6
```

327 + 458 = 785

First partition both numbers into **hundreds**, tens and ones.

Then add the ones. As there are more than 10 ones, we need to regroup 10 ones into 1 ten.

Next add the tens.

Finally combine the ones, tens and hundreds.

Now add the hundreds.

We can record this in columns.

```
  3 2 7
+ 4 5 8
    1 5
    7 0
  7 0 0
  7 8 5
```

leads to

```
  3 2 7
+ 4 5 8
  7 8 5
    1
```

$163 + 594 = \boxed{757}$

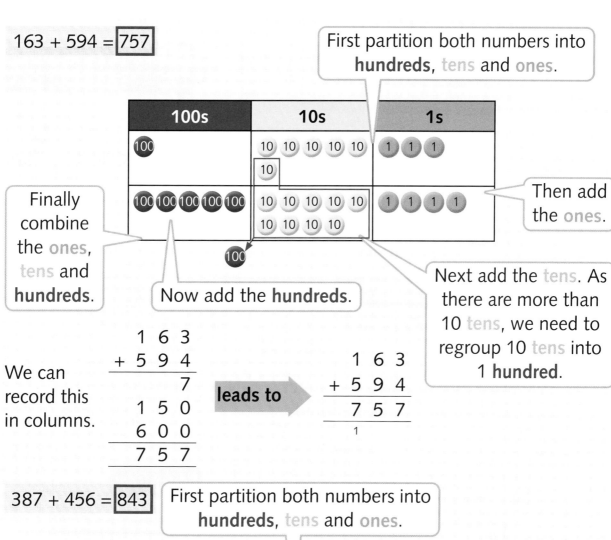

First partition both numbers into **hundreds**, tens and ones.

Then add the ones.

Next add the tens. As there are more than 10 tens, we need to regroup 10 tens into 1 **hundred**.

Finally combine the ones, tens and **hundreds**.

Now add the **hundreds**.

We can record this in columns.

```
  1 6 3
+ 5 9 4
───────
      7
  1 5 0
  6 0 0
───────
  7 5 7
```

leads to

```
  1 6 3
+ 5 9 4
───────
  7 5 7
    1
```

$387 + 456 = \boxed{843}$

First partition both numbers into **hundreds**, tens and ones.

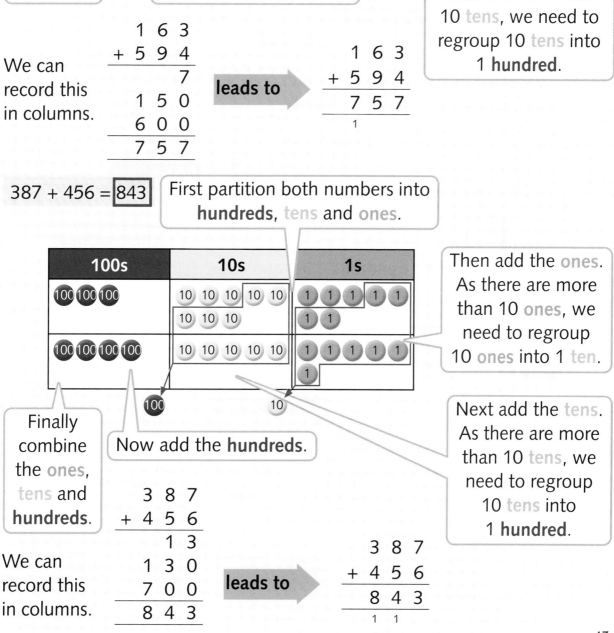

Then add the ones. As there are more than 10 ones, we need to regroup 10 ones into 1 ten.

Next add the tens. As there are more than 10 tens, we need to regroup 10 tens into 1 **hundred**.

Finally combine the ones, tens and **hundreds**.

Now add the **hundreds**.

We can record this in columns.

```
  3 8 7
+ 4 5 6
───────
    1 3
  1 3 0
  7 0 0
───────
  8 4 3
```

leads to

```
  3 8 7
+ 4 5 6
───────
  8 4 3
  1 1
```

Subtract two 3-digit numbers

Pages 6-11, 14-15, 22-25, 28-29, 32-37, 40-41

To subtract two 3-digit numbers, such as 587 − 235 or 732 − 486, we need to partition 3-digit numbers into hundreds, tens and ones and have instant recall of the subtraction facts to 20.

587 − 235 = 352

First partition 587 into **hundreds**, tens and ones.

Then subtract the ones.

⚠ **ALWAYS:**
Estimate
Calculate
Check

Finally place the partitioned number back together.

Now subtract the **hundreds**.

Next subtract the tens.

100s	10s	1s

We can record this in columns.

```
  500   80    7
−  200   30    5
  300   50    2
```

300 + 50 + 2 = 352

leads to

```
  5 8 7
− 2 3 5
  3 5 2
```

862 − 518 = 344

First partition 862 into **hundreds**, tens and ones.

Then subtract the ones. There are 2 ones in 862, and we need to subtract 8 ones. As there aren't enough ones in 862, exchange 1 ten for 10 ones.

100s	10s	1s

Finally place the partitioned number back together.

Now subtract the **hundreds**.

Next subtract the tens.

You can also write the exchanged values like this.

We can record this in columns.

```
        50   12
  800   6̶0   2̶
−  500   10    8
  300   40    4
```

300 + 40 + 4 = 344

leads to

```
     5 1
  8 6̶ 2
− 5 1 8
  3 4 4
```

```
     5 12
  8 6̶ 2̶
− 5 1 8
  3 4 4
```

44

 636 – 372 = **264**

First partition 636 into **hundreds**, tens and ones.

100s	10s	1s
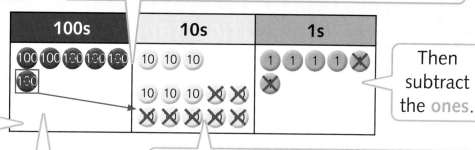		

Then subtract the ones.

Finally place the partitioned number back together.

Now subtract the **hundreds**.

Next subtract the tens. There are 3 tens in 636, and we need to subtract 7 tens. As there aren't enough tens in 636, exchange 1 **hundred** for 10 tens.

We can record this in columns.

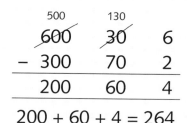

$$
\begin{array}{r}
{\scriptstyle 500} \quad {\scriptstyle 130} \\
\cancel{600} \quad \cancel{30} \quad 6 \\
- \;\;300 \quad\;\; 70 \quad\;\; 2 \\
\hline
200 \quad\;\; 60 \quad\;\; 4
\end{array}
$$

200 + 60 + 4 = 264

leads to

$$
\begin{array}{r}
{\scriptstyle 5}\;\;{\scriptstyle 1} \\
\cancel{6}\; 3\; 6 \\
-\; 3\; 7\; 2 \\
\hline
2\; 6\; 4
\end{array}
\qquad
\begin{array}{r}
{\scriptstyle 5}\;\;{\scriptstyle 13} \\
\cancel{6}\; \cancel{3}\; 6 \\
-\; 3\; 7\; 2 \\
\hline
2\; 6\; 4
\end{array}
$$

You can also write the exchanged values like this.

732 – 486 = **246**

First partition 732 into **hundreds**, tens and ones.

100s	10s	1s
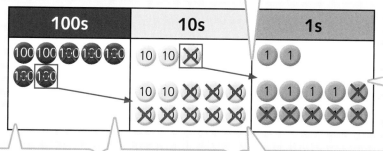		

Then subtract the ones. There are 2 ones in 732, and we need to subtract 6 ones. As there aren't enough ones in 732, exchange 1 ten for 10 ones.

Finally place the partitioned number back together.

Now subtract the **hundreds**.

Next subtract the tens. There are 3 tens in 732, and we need to subtract 8 tens. As there aren't enough tens in 732, exchange 1 **hundred** for 10 tens.

We can record this in columns.

$$
\begin{array}{r}
{\scriptstyle 600} \quad {\scriptstyle 120} \quad {\scriptstyle 12} \\
\cancel{700} \quad \cancel{30} \quad \cancel{2} \\
- \;\;400 \quad\;\; 80 \quad\;\; 6 \\
\hline
200 \quad\;\; 40 \quad\;\; 6
\end{array}
$$

200 + 40 + 6 = 246

leads to

You can also write the exchanged values like this.

$$
\begin{array}{r}
{\scriptstyle 6}\;\;{\scriptstyle 12}\;\;{\scriptstyle 1} \\
\cancel{7}\; \cancel{3}\; 2 \\
-\; 4\; 8\; 6 \\
\hline
2\; 4\; 6
\end{array}
\qquad
\begin{array}{r}
{\scriptstyle 6}\;\;{\scriptstyle 12}\;\;{\scriptstyle 12} \\
\cancel{7}\; \cancel{3}\; \cancel{2} \\
-\; 4\; 8\; 6 \\
\hline
2\; 4\; 6
\end{array}
$$

2, 5 and 10 multiplication tables

Pages 6-7

We can use the patterns of counting in steps of 2, 5 and 10 to recall the 2, 5 and 10 multiplication table facts and the related division facts.

We can **count on in 2s** to find out how many wheels there are.

We can write this as a multiplication **number sentence**: $4 \times 2 = 8$

4 **lots** of 2 is 8.

4 **multiplied** by 2 is 8.

We can say:

The **product** of 4 and 2 is 8.

4 **times** 2 is 8.

Four **2s** are 8.

Multiplication and **division** are related. They are **inverse operations**.

That means that they are **opposite operations** – multiplication **reverses** division, and division reverses multiplication.

We can use the **inverse relationship** between multiplication and division to help us recall the 2 **multiplication table facts** and the related **division facts**.

As a division we can say:

8 **divided by** 2 is 4.

We can write this as: $8 \div 2 = 4$

We can use a number line to recall the 2 multiplication table facts and related division facts.

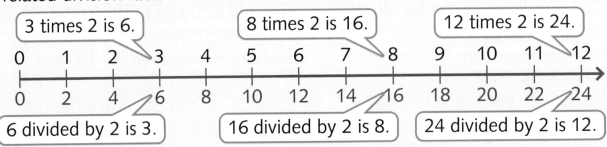

3 times 2 is 6.

8 times 2 is 16.

12 times 2 is 24.

6 divided by 2 is 3.

16 divided by 2 is 8.

24 divided by 2 is 12.

The **products** of the 2 multiplication table are called the **multiples of 2**.

So, 2, 4, 6, 8, 10, 12 and 14 are all multiples of 2.

What other multiples of 2 do you know?

We can **count on in 5s** to find out how many fingers there are.

5 10 15 20 25 30

There are 6 **groups of** 5 fingers.
There are 30 fingers **altogether**.

We can write this as a multiplication number sentence: $6 \times 5 = 30$

6 lots of 5 is 30.   The product of 6 and 5 is 30.   As a division we can say:

We can say: 6 multiplied by 5 is 30.   30 divided by 5 is 6.

We can write this as: $30 \div 5 = 6$

We can use a number line to recall the
5 multiplication and division facts.

2 times 5 is 10.

The products of the 5 multiplication
table are called the **multiples of 5**.

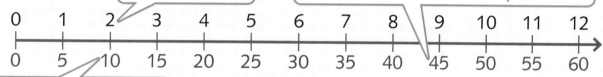

0   1   2   3   4   5   6   7   8   9   10   11   12

0   5   10   15   20   25   30   35   40   45   50   55   60

10 divided by 5 is 2.

10   20   30   40

We can **count on in 10s** to find out how
many pens there are.

There are 4 groups of 10 pens. There are 40 pens altogether.

We can write this as a multiplication number sentence: $4 \times 10 = 40$

4 times 10 is 40.   4 multiplied by 10 is 40.

We can say: Four 10s are 40.   As a division we can say:

40 divided by 10 is 4.

We can write this as: $40 \div 10 = 4$

We can use a number line to recall the
10 multiplication and division facts.

3 times 10 is 30.

The products of the 10 multiplication
table are called the **multiples of 10**.

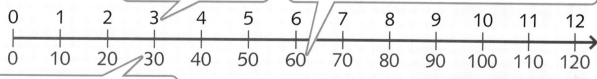

0   1   2   3   4   5   6   7   8   9   10   11   12

0   10   20   30   40   50   60   70   80   90   100   110   120

30 divided by 10 is 3.

Pages 48-59, 66-69

3 multiplication table

Pages 6–7, 46–47

We can use the pattern of counting in steps of 3 to recall the 3 multiplication table facts and the related division facts.

How many cubes are there **altogether**?

We can **count on in 3s** to find out how many cubes there are.

There are 7 groups of 3 cubes. There are 21 cubes altogether.

| 1 **group of** 3 is 3. | 3 groups of 3 are 9. | 5 groups of 3 are 15. | 7 groups of 3 are 21. |

0   3   6   9   12   15   18   21   24   27   30   33   36

2 groups of 3 are 6.   4 groups of 3 are 12.   6 groups of 3 are 18.

We can also write this as a **multiplication** calculation: $7 \times 3 = 21$

One 3 is 3.

$1 \times 3 = 3$

7 lots of 3 is 21.   7 times 3 is 21.   Seven **3s** are 21.

Two 3s are 6.

$2 \times 3 = 6$

7 **multiplied by** 3 is 21.

We can say:

The **product** of 7 and 3 is 21.

Three 3s are 9.

$3 \times 3 = 9$

The products of the 3 multiplication table are called the **multiples of 3**.

Four 3s are 12.

$4 \times 3 = 12$

Five 3s are 15.

$5 \times 3 = 15$

We can use the inverse relationship between multiplication and division to help us recall the 3 multiplication table facts and the related division facts.

Remember

There are 3 cubes in each tower.

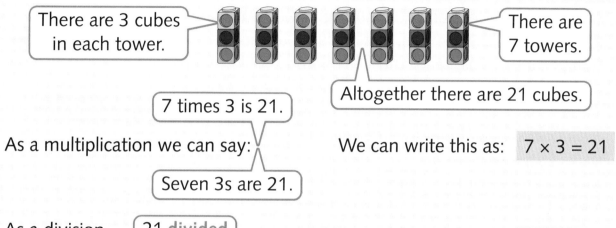

There are 7 towers.

Altogether there are 21 cubes.

7 times 3 is 21.

As a multiplication we can say:

Seven 3s are 21.

We can write this as: $7 \times 3 = 21$

As a division we can say:

21 divided by 3 is 7.

We can write this as: $21 \div 3 = 7$

We can use a number line to recall the 3 multiplication table facts and related division facts.

2 times 3 is 6.   5 times 3 is 15.   9 times 3 is 27.

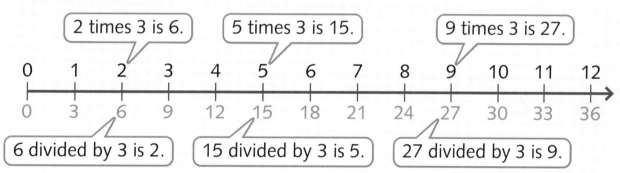

6 divided by 3 is 2.   15 divided by 3 is 5.   27 divided by 3 is 9.

Look at this 1–100 number square.

What patterns do you notice?

How can you use this number square to help you recall the 3 multiplication table facts and the related division facts?

1	2	3	4	5	6	7	8	9	10
11	12	13	14	15	16	17	18	19	20
21	22	23	24	25	26	27	28	29	30
31	32	33	34	35	36	37	38	39	40
41	42	43	44	45	46	47	48	49	50
51	52	53	54	55	56	57	58	59	60
61	62	63	64	65	66	67	68	69	70
71	72	73	74	75	76	77	78	79	80
81	82	83	84	85	86	87	88	89	90
91	92	93	94	95	96	97	98	99	100

Pages 50-59, 66-69

4 multiplication table

Pages 6-7, 20-21, 46-49

We can use the pattern of counting in steps of 4 and our knowledge of the 2 multiplication table to recall the 4 multiplication table facts and the related division facts.

How many dots are there **altogether**?

We can **count on in 4s** to find out how many dots there are.

> There are 6 groups of 4 dots. There are 24 dots altogether.

| 1 **group of** 4 is 4. | 3 groups of 4 are 12. | 5 groups of 4 are 20. |

0   4   8   12   16   20   24   28   32   36   40   44   48

| 2 groups of 4 are 8. | 4 groups of 4 are 16. | 6 groups of 4 are 24. |

We can also write this as a **multiplication** calculation: $6 \times 4 = 24$

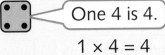 One 4 is 4.

$1 \times 4 = 4$

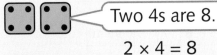 Two 4s are 8.

$2 \times 4 = 8$

Three 4s are 12.

$3 \times 4 = 12$

Four 4s are 16.

$4 \times 4 = 16$

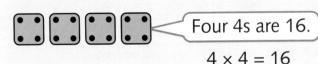 Five 4s are 20.

$5 \times 4 = 20$

| 6 **lots of** 4 is 24. | 6 **times** 4 is 24. | Six **4s** are 24. |

We can say:

6 **multiplied** by 4 is 24.

The **product** of 6 and 4 is 24.

The products of the 4 multiplication table are called the **multiples of 4**.

50

We can use the **inverse relationship** between multiplication and division to help us recall the 4 **multiplication table facts** and the related **division facts**.

 Remember

There are 4 dots on each dice.

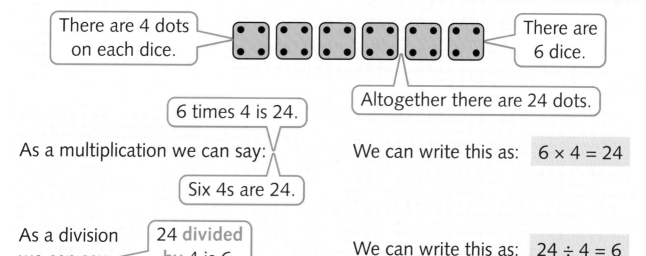

There are 6 dice.

Altogether there are 24 dots.

As a multiplication we can say:

6 times 4 is 24.

Six 4s are 24.

We can write this as: $6 \times 4 = 24$

As a division we can say:

24 **divided by** 4 is 6.

We can write this as: $24 \div 4 = 6$

We can use a number line to recall the 4 multiplication table facts and related division facts.

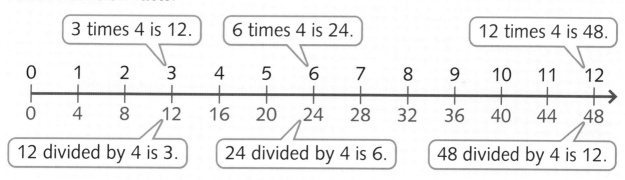

3 times 4 is 12.

6 times 4 is 24.

12 times 4 is 48.

12 divided by 4 is 3.

24 divided by 4 is 6.

48 divided by 4 is 12.

Look at this 1–100 number square.

What patterns do you notice?

What do you notice about the multiples of 4 and the **multiples of 2**?

What is the link between the 2 and 4 multiplication tables?

What is the link between multiplying by 4 and **doubling**?

1	2	3	4	5	6	7	8	9	10
11	12	13	14	15	16	17	18	19	20
21	22	23	24	25	26	27	28	29	30
31	32	33	34	35	36	37	38	39	40
41	42	43	44	45	46	47	48	49	50
51	52	53	54	55	56	57	58	59	60
61	62	63	64	65	66	67	68	69	70
71	72	73	74	75	76	77	78	79	80
81	82	83	84	85	86	87	88	89	90
91	92	93	94	95	96	97	98	99	100

Pages 52-59, 66-69

8 multiplication table

Pages 6-7, 20-21, 46-51

We can use the pattern of counting in steps of 8 and our knowledge of the 2 and 4 multiplication tables to recall the 8 multiplication table facts and the related division facts.

How many legs are there **altogether**?

We can **count on in 8s** to find out how many legs there are.

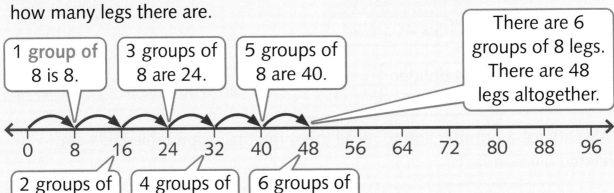

1 **group of** 8 is 8.

3 groups of 8 are 24.

5 groups of 8 are 40.

There are 6 groups of 8 legs. There are 48 legs altogether.

2 groups of 8 are 16.

4 groups of 8 are 32.

6 groups of 8 are 48.

0 8 16 24 32 40 48 56 64 72 80 88 96

We can also write this as a **multiplication** calculation: $6 \times 8 = 48$

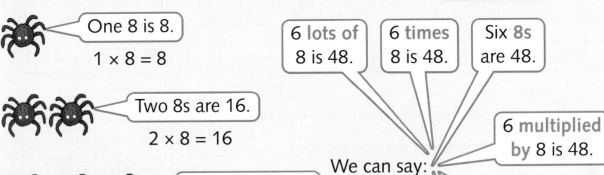

One 8 is 8.

$1 \times 8 = 8$

Two 8s are 16.

$2 \times 8 = 16$

Three 8s are 24.

$3 \times 8 = 24$

Four 8s are 32.

$4 \times 8 = 32$

Five 8s are 40.

$5 \times 8 = 40$

6 lots of 8 is 48.

6 times 8 is 48.

Six **8s** are 48.

We can say:

6 **multiplied by** 8 is 48.

The **product** of 6 and 8 is 48.

The products of the 8 multiplication table are called the **multiples of 8**.

We can use the **inverse relationship** between multiplication and division to help us recall the 8 **multiplication table facts** and the related **division facts**.

Each spider has 8 legs.

There are 6 spiders.

Altogether there are 48 legs.

As a multiplication we can say:

6 times 8 is 48.

Six 8s are 48.

We can write this as: $6 \times 8 = 48$

As a division we can say:

48 **divided** by 8 is 6.

We can write this as: $48 \div 8 = 6$

We can use a number line to recall the 8 multiplication table facts and related division facts.

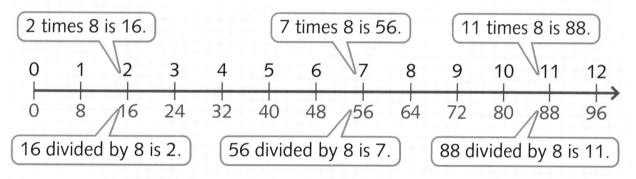

2 times 8 is 16.

7 times 8 is 56.

11 times 8 is 88.

16 divided by 8 is 2.

56 divided by 8 is 7.

88 divided by 8 is 11.

Look at these three number lines.

How are they the same? How are they different?

What patterns do you notice?

What is the link between the 2, 4 and 8 multiplication tables?

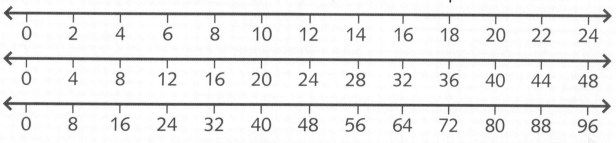

Pages 54-59, 66-69

53

Related multiplication and division facts

Pages 6-7, 46-53

Place value knowledge, understanding the relationship between multiplication and division, and recalling multiplication and division facts all help us to multiply and divide multiples of 10.

This **array** shows 4 **lots of** 5 chocolates.

$5 + 5 + 5 + 5 = 20$ ▷ $4 \times 5 = 20$ ▷

It also shows 5 lots of 4 chocolates.

$4 + 4 + 4 + 4 + 4 = 20$ ▷ $5 \times 4 = 20$ ▷

We can see from this array that:

4 lots of 5 = 5 lots of 4

$4 \times 5 = 5 \times 4$

An array shows us that multiplication can be done in any order – it's **commutative**.

We can use this **known fact** to work out that
5×4 tens $= 20$ tens
$5 \times 40 = 200$

We know that
$5 \times 4 = 20$

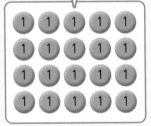

10 times larger ➡

$5 \times 4 = 20$

As one of the numbers in the calculation is 10 times larger, then …

… the answer is also 10 times larger.

$5 \times 40 = 200$

 Say

If $5 \times 4 = 20$ and $5 \times 40 = 200$, what is the answer to this calculation?

$50 \times 4 = \boxed{}$

How do you know?

Is this statement true or false? $40 \times 5 = 4 \times 50$

Explain why.

- Multiplication can be done in any order – it's commutative.
- Multiplication and division are related. If we know one multiplication or division fact, then we know three other related facts.

There are 20 tens.
20 tens divided into groups of 4 tens = 5
$200 \div 40 = 5$

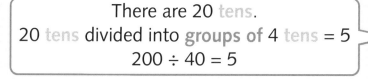

We can also see:
20 tens divided into 4 equal parts = 5 tens
$200 \div 4 = 50$

So, and and

| 20 | 200 | 200 |
| 5   4 | 5   40 | 50   4 |

$5 \times 4 = 20$	$5 \times 40 = 200$	$50 \times 4 = 200$
$4 \times 5 = 20$	$40 \times 5 = 200$	$4 \times 50 = 200$
$20 \div 4 = 5$	$200 \div 40 = 5$	$200 \div 4 = 50$
$20 \div 5 = 4$	$200 \div 5 = 40$	$200 \div 50 = 4$

 Write

What multiplication facts does this array show?

What are the related division facts?

 Write

What multiplication facts does this array show?

What are the related division facts?

What patterns do you notice about all your multiplication and division facts?

Pages 56–59

55

Multiply a 2-digit number by a 1-digit number

Pages 6–11, 22–23, 46–55

We can use our understanding of place value and multiplication table facts to multiply a 2-digit number by a 1-digit number, such as 43 × 2 or 36 × 4.

We can represent this multiplication **calculation** using place value counters.

⚠ **ALWAYS:**
Estimate
Calculate
Check

As we are multiplying 43 by 2, first **partition** 2 lots of 43 into tens and ones.

Then **multiply** the ones. 3 ones multiplied by 2 (3 × 2)

Next multiply the tens. 4 tens multiplied by 2 (40 × 2)

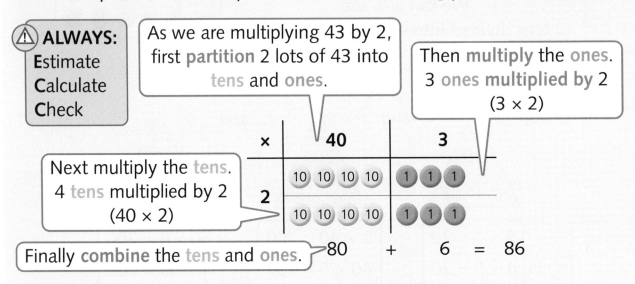

Finally **combine** the tens and ones.

80 + 6 = 86

We can record this calculation in different ways.

Grid method

×	40	3	
2	80	6	= 86

Partitioning method

43 × 2 = (40 × 2) + (3 × 2)
= 80 + 6
= 86

Expanded written method

```
    4 3
×     2
      6   (3 × 2)
    8 0   (40 × 2)
    8 6
```

leads to

Formal written method of short multiplication

```
    4 3
×     2
    8 6
```

What's the same about each of these methods?

What's different?

Which method do you prefer? Why?

$36 \times 4 = \boxed{144}$

Step 1: Set out the calculation.

As we are multiplying 36 by 4, first partition 4 lots of 36 into tens and ones.

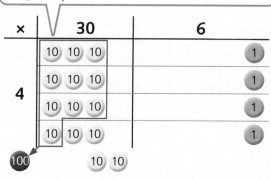

Step 2: Multiply the ones.

6 ones multiplied by 4 (6 × 4 = 24). As there are more than 10 ones we need to regroup 20 ones into 2 tens.

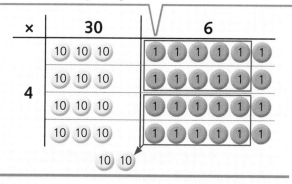

Step 3: Multiply the tens.

3 tens multiplied by 4 (30 × 4 = 120). As there are more than 10 tens we need to regroup 10 tens into 1 hundred.

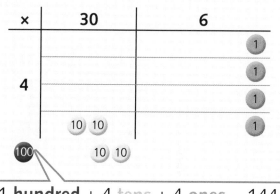

Step 4: Combine the hundreds, tens and ones.

1 hundred + 4 tens + 4 ones = 144
100 + 40 + 4 = 144

We can record this calculation in different ways.

Grid method

×	30	6
4	120	24	= 144

Partitioning method

36 × 4 = (30 × 4) + (6 × 4)
= 120 + 24
= 144

Expanded written method

```
    3 6
  ×   4
    2 4   (6 × 4)
  1 2 0   (30 × 4)
  1 4 4
```

leads to

Formal written method of short multiplication

```
    3 6          3 6
  ×   4        × 2 4
  1 4 4        1 4 4
      2
```

You can also write the regrouped value like this.

What's the same about each of these methods?

What's different?

Which method do you prefer? Why?

Divide a 2-digit number by a 1-digit number

Pages 6-11, 22-23, 46-55

We can use our understanding of place value and multiplication and division facts to divide a 2-digit number by a 1-digit number, such as $76 \div 2$.

Each part of a **division** calculation has a special name. It's helpful to know these names.

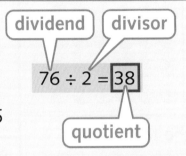

dividend   divisor

$76 \div 2 = \boxed{38}$

quotient

⚠ **ALWAYS:**
Estimate
Calculate
Check

We can **decompose** or **partition** 76 into **tens** and **ones**.

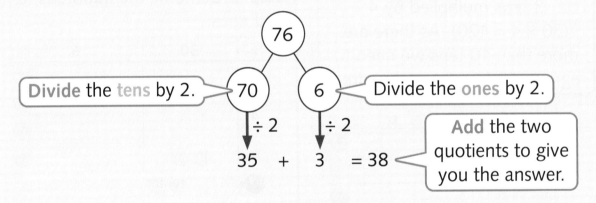

76

Divide the **tens** by 2. — 70   6 — **Divide** the **ones** by 2.

$\div 2$ $\div 2$

35 + 3 = 38

Add the two quotients to give you the answer.

Remember We can decompose (or **regroup**) numbers in different ways.

We can also regroup 76 like this.

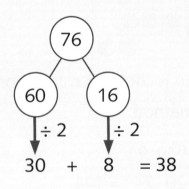

76

60   16

$\div 2$ $\div 2$

30 + 8 = 38

How else could you regroup 76 to work out the answer to this division calculation?

How does **halving** help when dividing 76 by 2?

How does halving help when dividing 76 by 4?

We can represent this with place value counters.

Step 1: Set out the calculation.

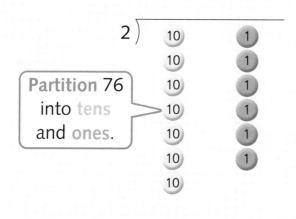

Partition 76 into tens and ones.

$$2 \overline{)7\ 6}$$

Step 2: Share the tens.

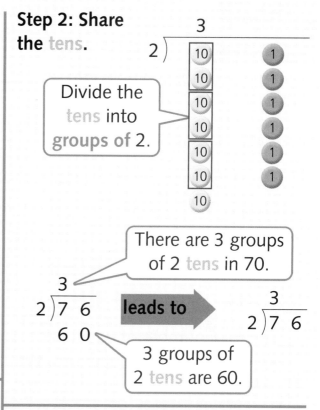

Divide the tens into groups of 2.

There are 3 groups of 2 tens in 70.

$$2 \overset{3}{\overline{)7\ 6}} \\ 6\ 0$$

leads to

$$2 \overset{3}{\overline{)7\ 6}}$$

3 groups of 2 tens are 60.

Step 3: Exchange the tens.

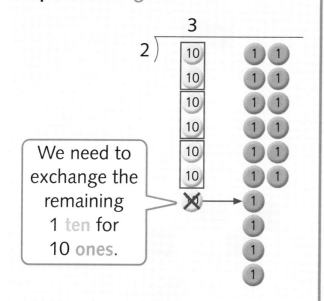

We need to exchange the remaining 1 ten for 10 ones.

$$2 \overset{3}{\overline{)7\ 6}} \\ -\ 6\ 0 \\ \overline{\quad 1\ 6}$$

leads to

$$2 \overset{3}{\overline{)7\ {}^16}}$$

There are now 16 ones.

Step 4: Share the ones.

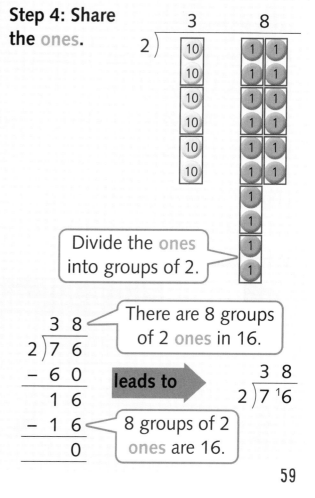

Divide the ones into groups of 2.

$$2 \overset{3\ \ 8}{\overline{)7\ 6}} \\ -\ 6\ 0 \\ \overline{\quad 1\ 6} \\ -\ 1\ 6 \\ \overline{\quad\quad 0}$$

There are 8 groups of 2 ones in 16.

leads to

$$2 \overset{3\ \ 8}{\overline{)7\ {}^16}}$$

8 groups of 2 ones are 16.

Tenths

When we divide a whole into 10 equal parts, each of the parts is a tenth.

This shape represents 1 **whole**.

It has been **divided into** 10 **equal parts**.

Each square is 1 out of 10 equal squares.

It shows 1 **part** shaded.

So, the shaded part is one-**tenth**.

We can write one-**tenth** as a **fraction**.

The total number of equal parts a whole has been divided into. We call this number the **denominator**.

The number of parts we are thinking about. We call this number the **numerator**.

$\dfrac{1}{10}$

We call this line the **division bar** or the **vinculum**.

Look at this shape.

It has been divided into 10 equal parts.

It shows 3 parts shaded.

So, three-**tenths** of this shape is shaded.

We can write this as $\frac{3}{10}$.

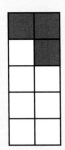

Look at these shapes.

What's the same about all the shapes?

What's different?

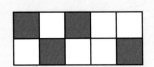

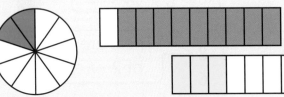

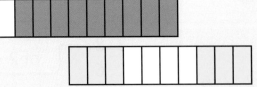

What about this shape?

 What fraction of each shape is shaded?

 How would you write it as a fraction?

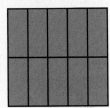

One-**tenth** or $\frac{1}{10}$ of this shape is shaded.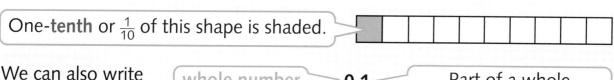

We can also write one-**tenth** as a **decimal**.

whole number → **0·1** ← Part of a whole (fractional part) – **tenth**

decimal point

We say: ← zero point one

Just like whole numbers, we can also write decimals using a place value grid.

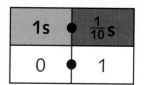

 Say

 Write

Look at the shapes on page 60.

How would you say and write each of these as a decimal?

Also, like whole numbers, we can position **tenths** on a number line and count on and back in **tenths**.

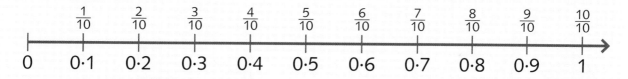

 Say

Look at the fractions above the number line.

- Count on in **tenths** from 0 to 1.
- Count back in **tenths** from 1 to 0.
- Starting from a **tenth** such as $\frac{2}{10}$, count on in **tenths** to 1.
- Starting from a **tenth** such as $\frac{8}{10}$, count back in **tenths** to 0.

Look at the decimals below the number line.

Count on and back in **tenths**.

- Count on in **tenths** as fractions beyond 1.
- Count on in **tenths** as decimals beyond 1.
- Count back from 3 in **tenths** as fractions and as decimals.

Pages 62–77

Unit fractions

Pages 60-61

A unit fraction is a fraction that represents 1 equal part of a whole.

A half, one-third and one-quarter are all unit fractions.

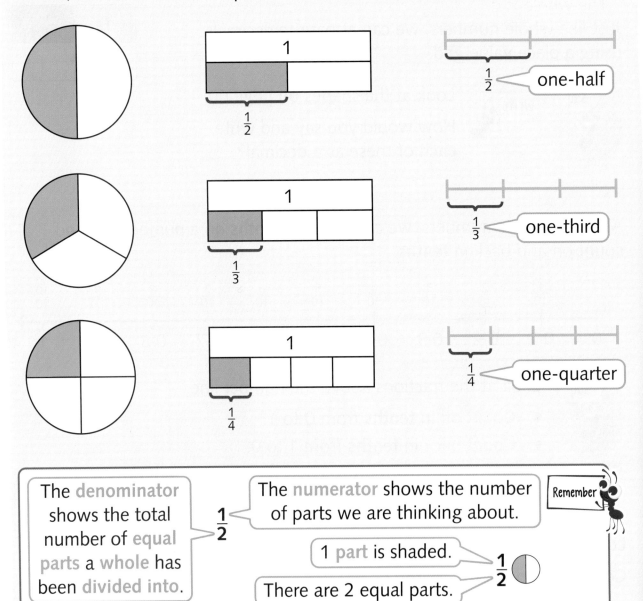

The denominator shows the total number of equal parts a whole has been divided into.

The numerator shows the number of parts we are thinking about.

$\frac{1}{2}$

1 part is shaded.

There are 2 equal parts.

$\frac{1}{2}$

Remember

What's the same about the fractions on this page?

What's different?

What can you say about unit fractions?

Unit fractions can also be used to represent one part of a group of objects.

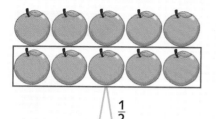

$\frac{1}{2}$

The whole is divided into 2 equal parts. One of the parts is one-half of the whole.

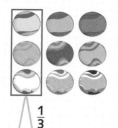

$\frac{1}{3}$

The whole is divided into 3 equal parts. One of the parts is one-third of the whole.

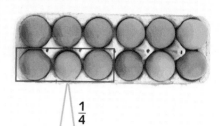

$\frac{1}{4}$

The whole is divided into 4 equal parts. One of the parts is one-quarter of the whole.

This diagram is called a fraction wall. It shows different unit fractions.

What do you notice about the denominators as you move down the diagram?

What do you notice about the size of the shaded part as you move down the diagram?

What can you say about the relationship between the size of the denominator and the size of the part of the whole?

1									

$\frac{1}{2}$	
$\frac{1}{3}$		
$\frac{1}{4}$			
$\frac{1}{5}$				
$\frac{1}{6}$					
$\frac{1}{7}$						
$\frac{1}{8}$							
$\frac{1}{9}$								
$\frac{1}{10}$									

Say Point to each cake and say the unit fraction.

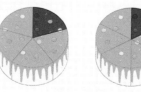

Pages 64-77

Non-unit fractions

Pages 60–63

A non-unit fraction is a fraction that represents more than 1 equal part of a whole.

Each of these circles has been **divided into** 4 **equal parts**.

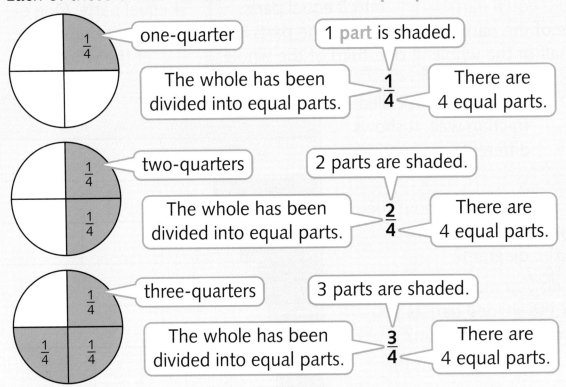

one-quarter

$\frac{1}{4}$

The whole has been divided into equal parts.

1 **part** is shaded.

$\frac{1}{4}$

There are 4 equal parts.

two-quarters

$\frac{1}{4}$

$\frac{1}{4}$

The whole has been divided into equal parts.

2 parts are shaded.

$\frac{2}{4}$

There are 4 equal parts.

three-quarters

$\frac{1}{4}$

$\frac{1}{4}$

$\frac{1}{4}$

The whole has been divided into equal parts.

3 parts are shaded.

$\frac{3}{4}$

There are 4 equal parts.

Look at this model. It has been divided into 10 equal parts.

Each part is one-**tenth**.

2 one-**tenths** or 2 **tenths** ($\frac{2}{10}$) are shaded green.

3 one-**tenths** or 3 **tenths** ($\frac{3}{10}$) are shaded blue.

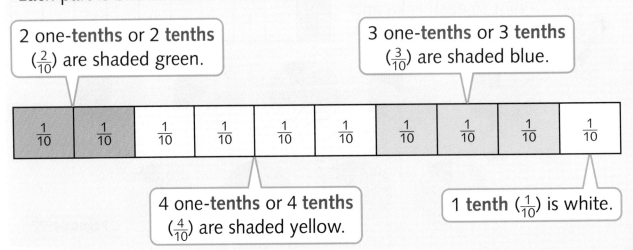

| $\frac{1}{10}$ | $\frac{1}{10}$ | $\frac{1}{10}$ | $\frac{1}{10}$ | $\frac{1}{10}$ | $\frac{1}{10}$ | $\frac{1}{10}$ | $\frac{1}{10}$ | $\frac{1}{10}$ | $\frac{1}{10}$ |

4 one-**tenths** or 4 **tenths** ($\frac{4}{10}$) are shaded yellow.

1 **tenth** ($\frac{1}{10}$) is white.

Look at these shapes and groups of objects.

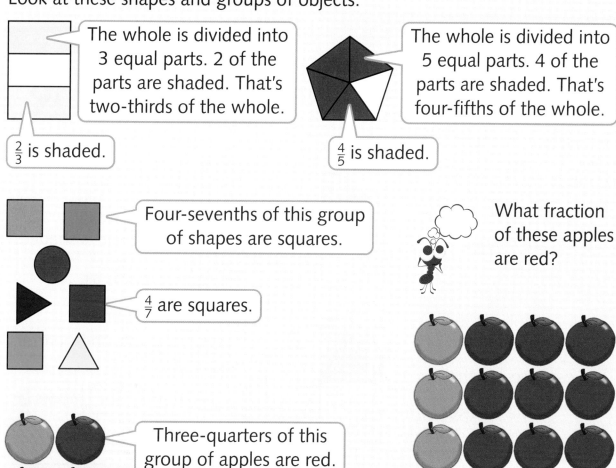

The whole is divided into 3 equal parts. 2 of the parts are shaded. That's two-thirds of the whole.

$\frac{2}{3}$ is shaded.

The whole is divided into 5 equal parts. 4 of the parts are shaded. That's four-fifths of the whole.

$\frac{4}{5}$ is shaded.

Four-sevenths of this group of shapes are squares.

$\frac{4}{7}$ are squares.

What fraction of these apples are red?

Three-quarters of this group of apples are red.

$\frac{3}{4}$ are red.

Say We can represent non-unit fractions on a number line.

Use the number lines to count on and back.

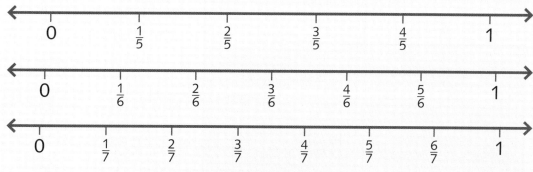

Say Look at the number lines above.

- Count on in fractions beyond 1.
- Count back in fractions from 3.

Pages 66-77

Equivalent fractions

Pages 46–53, 60–65

The same fraction can be described in different ways – for example, one-half is equal to two-quarters. These related fractions are called equivalent fractions.

Look at this circle.

There are 12 **equal parts**.

3 **parts** are shaded.

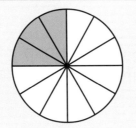

We can say that:

Three-twelfths of the circle is shaded.

We can write this as: $\frac{3}{12}$

Look carefully at the circle again.

We can also see that:

One-quarter of the circle is shaded.

$\frac{1}{4}$

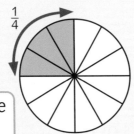

Three-twelfths is **equivalent** to one-quarter.

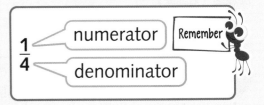

$\frac{1}{4}$ numerator Remember

denominator

Equivalent fractions are fractions that have the **same value**.

They have different **numerators** and **denominators**.

Look at these fraction walls.

1			
$\frac{1}{2}$		$\frac{1}{2}$	
$\frac{1}{4}$	$\frac{1}{4}$	$\frac{1}{4}$	$\frac{1}{4}$

This fraction wall shows that:

$\frac{1}{2} = \frac{2}{4}$

One-half is equivalent to two-quarters.

1					
$\frac{1}{3}$		$\frac{1}{3}$		$\frac{1}{3}$	
$\frac{1}{6}$	$\frac{1}{6}$	$\frac{1}{6}$	$\frac{1}{6}$	$\frac{1}{6}$	$\frac{1}{6}$
$\frac{1}{12}$ $\frac{1}{12}$	$\frac{1}{12}$ $\frac{1}{12}$	$\frac{1}{12}$ $\frac{1}{12}$	$\frac{1}{12}$ $\frac{1}{12}$	$\frac{1}{12}$ $\frac{1}{12}$	$\frac{1}{12}$ $\frac{1}{12}$

This fraction wall shows that:

$\frac{1}{3} = \frac{2}{6} = \frac{4}{12}$

One-third is equivalent to two-sixths, which is equivalent to four-twelfths.

Look at these two fraction walls.

How are they the same?

How are they different?

Say What equivalent fractions can you identify from these fraction walls?

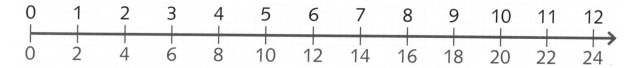

1											
$\frac{1}{2}$						$\frac{1}{2}$					
$\frac{1}{4}$			$\frac{1}{4}$			$\frac{1}{4}$			$\frac{1}{4}$		
$\frac{1}{8}$		$\frac{1}{8}$		$\frac{1}{8}$		$\frac{1}{8}$		$\frac{1}{8}$	$\frac{1}{8}$	$\frac{1}{8}$	$\frac{1}{8}$
$\frac{1}{12}$	$\frac{1}{12}$	$\frac{1}{12}$	$\frac{1}{12}$	$\frac{1}{12}$	$\frac{1}{12}$	$\frac{1}{12}$	$\frac{1}{12}$	$\frac{1}{12}$	$\frac{1}{12}$	$\frac{1}{12}$	$\frac{1}{12}$

1									
$\frac{1}{5}$		$\frac{1}{5}$		$\frac{1}{5}$		$\frac{1}{5}$		$\frac{1}{5}$	
$\frac{1}{10}$	$\frac{1}{10}$	$\frac{1}{10}$	$\frac{1}{10}$	$\frac{1}{10}$	$\frac{1}{10}$	$\frac{1}{10}$	$\frac{1}{10}$	$\frac{1}{10}$	$\frac{1}{10}$

Look at this number line.

0	1	2	3	4	5	6	7	8	9	10	11	12
0	2	4	6	8	10	12	14	16	18	20	22	24

What do you notice?

Where have you seen this number line before?

We can use this number line to identify fractions that are equivalent to $\frac{1}{2}$.

Say Use these number lines to identify other equivalent fractions.

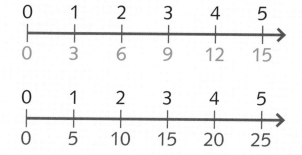

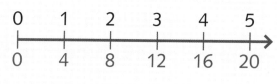

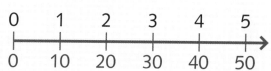

Calculate a fraction of an amount

Pages 46–53, 60–65

We can find a fraction of an amount by dividing the amount into equal groups.

$\frac{1}{5}$ of 15 = $\boxed{3}$

To find one-fifth of a group of objects:

1. Count the total number of objects – the whole.

2. Divide the whole into 5 equal groups.

3. Count the number of objects in 1 group.

We can show this in a model.

15 is the whole.

The whole has been divided into 5 equal groups.

15

1 group is one-fifth of the whole.

We can say: 15 divided into 5 equal groups is equal to 3.

$\frac{1}{5}$ numerator | Remember
denominator

We can also say: One-fifth of 15 is equal to 3.

When calculating a fraction of an amount, the denominator of the fraction tells us how many equal groups the whole is divided into.

Divide the whole into 5 equal groups. $\frac{1}{5}$

The numerator of the fraction tells us how many groups of the whole we are finding.

Find the amount in 1 of the groups.

So, to find $\frac{1}{5}$ of 15, divide 15 by 5. $15 \div 5 = 3$

 Draw Draw models to find:

$\frac{1}{3}$ of 18 = $\boxed{}$ $\frac{1}{6}$ of 54 = $\boxed{}$ $\frac{1}{4}$ of 32 = $\boxed{}$

$\frac{2}{5}$ of 15 = 6   What is the same and what is different about $\frac{1}{5}$ and $\frac{2}{5}$?

To find two-fifths of a group of objects:

1. Count the total number of objects – the whole.

2. Divide the whole into 5 equal groups.

3. Count the number of objects in 2 groups.

We can show this in a model.

15 is the whole.

The whole has been divided into 5 equal groups.

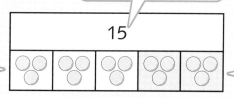

15

2 groups are two-fifths of the whole.

We can say:
15 divided into 5 equal groups is equal to 3.
2 groups of 3 is equal to 6.

We can also say: Two-fifths of 15 is equal to 6.

The **quotient** is the answer to a **division** calculation. Remember

So, to find $\frac{2}{5}$ of 15:

- First, divide 15 by 5 to find $\frac{1}{5}$.

$15 \div 5 = 3$

Divide the whole into 5 equal groups.

$\dfrac{2}{5}$

Find the amount in 2 of the groups.

- Then **multiply** the quotient by 2 to find the answer.

$3 \times 2 = 6$

 Draw   Draw models to find:

$\frac{2}{3}$ of 18 = ☐ $\frac{5}{6}$ of 54 = ☐ $\frac{3}{4}$ of 32 = ☐

69

Compare fractions

Pages 60-65

Just as with whole numbers, we can compare two fractions, saying which is larger and which is smaller. We can use the symbols > and < to compare fractions.

Look at this fraction wall. We can use it to help us **compare** two fractions.

Which row has the fewest **equal parts**?

> When the **whole** is the **same**, the **fewer** the number of equal parts, the **larger** each equal part is.

Which row has the most equal parts?

> When the whole is the same, the **greater** the number of equal parts, the **smaller** each equal part is.

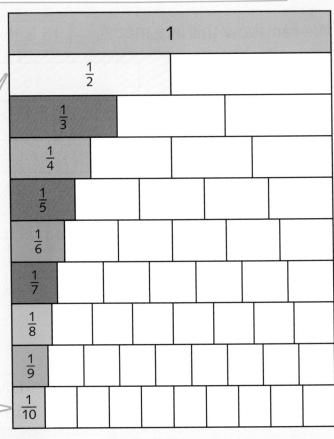

Look at these two **unit fractions**: $\frac{1}{2}$ $\frac{1}{10}$

The fraction wall shows that:

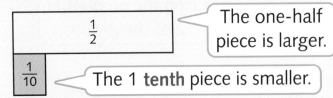

> The one-half piece is larger.

> The 1 **tenth** piece is smaller.

A unit fraction represents 1 equal part of a whole.

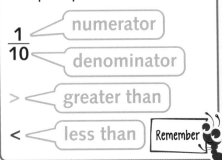

$\frac{1}{10}$

— numerator
— denominator
> — greater than
< — less than | Remember

Look at the denominator in each fraction: $\frac{1}{2}$ $\frac{1}{10}$

When **comparing** unit fractions, the greater the denominator, the smaller the fraction.

We can write: $\frac{1}{2} > \frac{1}{10}$

$\frac{1}{10} < \frac{1}{2}$

So, we can say that:

> One-half is greater than 1 **tenth**.

> 1 **tenth** is less than one-half.

Look at these two fractions: $\frac{3}{10}$ $\frac{9}{10}$

What's the same? What's different?

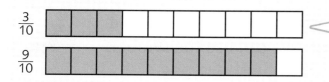

A **non-unit fraction** represents more than 1 equal part of a whole. Remember

$\frac{3}{10}$ These models have both been divided into **tenths**. Both fractions have the **same denominator**.

$\frac{9}{10}$

To compare fractions with the same denominator, we look at the **numerators**.

We can see from the models above that there are more shaded parts in 9 **tenths** than in 3 **tenths**.

When comparing fractions with the same denominator, the greater the numerator, the greater the fraction.

So, we can say that: 9 **tenths** is greater than 3 **tenths**. We can write:

3 **tenths** is less than 9 **tenths**.

$\frac{9}{10} > \frac{3}{10}$

$\frac{3}{10} < \frac{9}{10}$

 Say   Use the number lines below to compare unit fractions and fractions with the same denominator.

 Write   Use the < and > symbols to write statements comparing pairs of fractions.

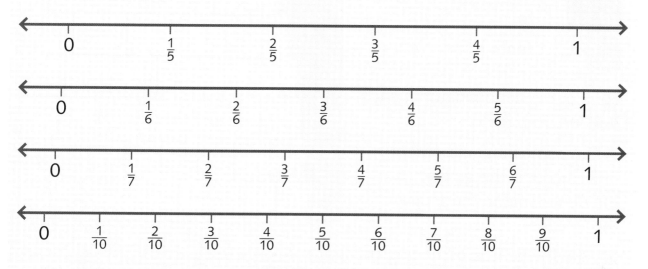

Pages 72-73

Order fractions

Pages 60-65, 70-71

Just as with whole numbers, we can order a set of fractions from smallest to largest or largest to smallest. We can use the symbols > and < to order fractions.

We can order a set of fractions:

- in ascending order – from smallest to largest
- or in descending order – from largest to smallest.

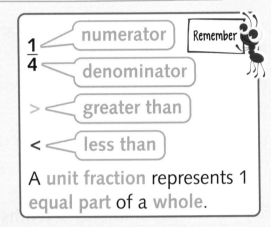

$\frac{1}{4}$ — numerator
— denominator

Remember

> — greater than

< — less than

A unit fraction represents 1 equal part of a whole.

A fraction wall can help us order fractions.

Look at this set of unit fractions:

$\frac{1}{6}$ $\frac{1}{2}$ $\frac{1}{10}$ $\frac{1}{4}$

The fraction wall shows:

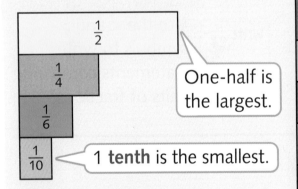

One-half is the largest.

1 **tenth** is the smallest.

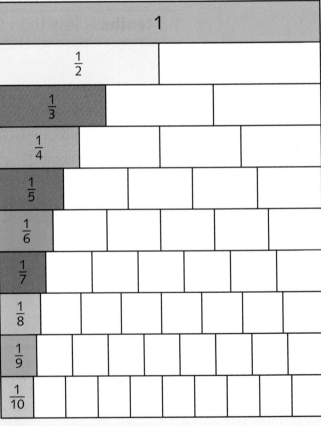

Look at the denominator in each fraction: $\frac{1}{6}$ $\frac{1}{2}$ $\frac{1}{10}$ $\frac{1}{4}$

When comparing and ordering unit fractions, the greater the denominator, the smaller the fraction.

So, the fractions in ascending order are: $\frac{1}{10} < \frac{1}{6} < \frac{1}{4} < \frac{1}{2}$

The fractions in descending order are: $\frac{1}{2} > \frac{1}{4} > \frac{1}{6} > \frac{1}{10}$

Look at this set of fractions:

$\frac{3}{8}$ $\frac{1}{8}$ $\frac{7}{8}$ $\frac{5}{8}$

What's the same?

A **non-unit fraction** represents more than 1 equal part of a whole.

Remember

What's different?

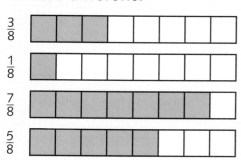

These bar models have all been divided into eighths. All the fractions have the **same denominator**.

$\frac{3}{8}$

$\frac{1}{8}$

$\frac{7}{8}$

$\frac{5}{8}$

To compare and order fractions with the same denominator, we look at the numerators.

We can see from the models above that seven-eighths has the most shaded parts and one-eighth has the fewest shaded parts.

So, the fractions in ascending order are: $\frac{1}{8} < \frac{3}{8} < \frac{5}{8} < \frac{7}{8}$

The fractions in descending order are: $\frac{7}{8} > \frac{5}{8} > \frac{3}{8} > \frac{1}{8}$

Just like with whole numbers, we can use number lines to order unit fractions and fractions with the same denominator.

0 $\frac{1}{10}$ $\frac{1}{6}$ $\frac{1}{4}$ $\frac{1}{2}$ 1   0 $\frac{1}{8}$ $\frac{3}{8}$ $\frac{5}{8}$ $\frac{7}{8}$ 1

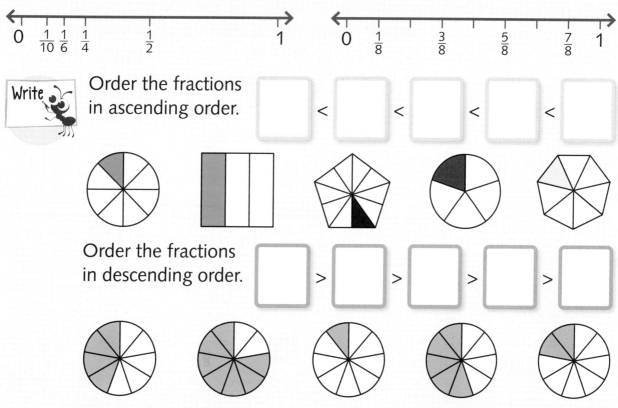

Write

Order the fractions in ascending order.

☐ < ☐ < ☐ < ☐ < ☐

Order the fractions in descending order.

☐ > ☐ > ☐ > ☐ > ☐

Place each set of ordered fractions on a number line.

73

Add fractions

Pages 22-23, 60-65

Adding fractions with the same denominator is like adding whole numbers. We add the numerators and write the total over the same denominator.

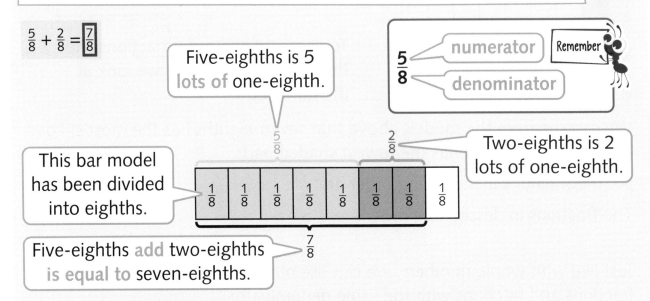

$\frac{5}{8} + \frac{2}{8} = \frac{7}{8}$

Five-eighths is 5 lots of one-eighth.

numerator   Remember

$\frac{5}{8}$

denominator

$\frac{5}{8}$

This bar model has been divided into eighths.

| $\frac{1}{8}$ | $\frac{1}{8}$ | $\frac{1}{8}$ | $\frac{1}{8}$ | $\frac{1}{8}$ | $\frac{1}{8}$ | $\frac{1}{8}$ | $\frac{1}{8}$ |

$\frac{2}{8}$

Two-eighths is 2 lots of one-eighth.

$\frac{7}{8}$

Five-eighths add two-eighths is equal to seven-eighths.

When fractions have the same denominator, we call this a common denominator. When we add fractions with a common denominator, the denominators stay the same because they tell you the total number of parts in the whole. The total number of parts does not change.

We just add the numerators to find out how many parts of the whole there are altogether.

We can show addition of fractions with a common denominator on a number line.

$+ \frac{2}{8}$

0    $\frac{1}{8}$ $\frac{2}{8}$ $\frac{3}{8}$ $\frac{4}{8}$ $\frac{5}{8}$ $\frac{6}{8}$ $\frac{7}{8}$ 1

Remember to always use what you know to help work out what you don't know.

So, if we know that 5 + 2 = 7, then we also know that: $\frac{5}{8} + \frac{2}{8} = \frac{7}{8}$

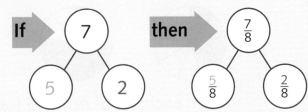

Commutativity works the same with fractions as it does with whole numbers.

That means that:

$$\frac{5}{8} + \frac{2}{8} = \frac{7}{8}$$ and

Addition can be done in any order – it's commutative. **Remember**

$$\frac{2}{8} + \frac{5}{8} = \frac{7}{8}$$

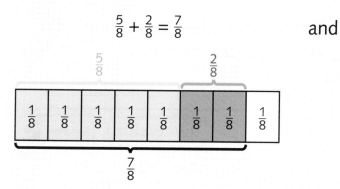

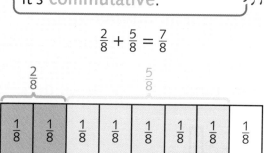

Just like with whole numbers, we can also add more than two fractions.

What changes when you add these three fractions?

What stays the same?

$$\frac{2}{12} + \frac{7}{12} + \frac{1}{12} = \boxed{\frac{10}{12}}$$

This model has been divided into twelfths.

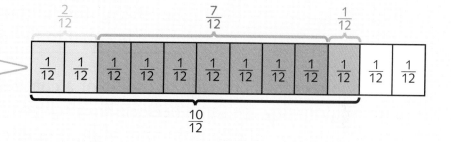

We can say: Two-twelfths add seven-twelfths add one-twelfth is equal to ten-twelfths.

Draw   **Write**   Draw models or use number lines to work out these fraction addition calculations.

$$\frac{3}{7} + \frac{2}{7} = \boxed{}$$ $$\frac{1}{9} + \frac{3}{9} + \frac{4}{9} = \boxed{}$$

$$\frac{4}{10} + \boxed{} = \frac{9}{10}$$ $$\frac{3}{8} + \boxed{} + \frac{2}{8} = \frac{6}{8}$$

Pages 75-76

Subtract fractions

Pages 22-23, 60-65, 74-75

Subtracting fractions with the same denominator is like subtracting whole numbers. We subtract the numerators and write the difference over the same denominator.

$\frac{7}{8} - \frac{2}{8} = \boxed{\frac{5}{8}}$

numerator

Remember

$\frac{7}{8}$

denominator

The result of a subtraction is called the difference.

Seven-eighths is 7 lots of one-eighth.

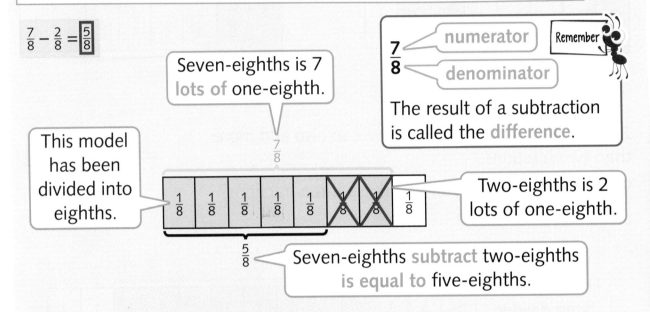

This model has been divided into eighths.

Two-eighths is 2 lots of one-eighth.

Seven-eighths subtract two-eighths is equal to five-eighths.

When we subtract fractions with the same or a common denominator, the denominators stay the same because they tell you the total number of parts in the whole. The total number of parts does not change.

We just subtract the numerators to find out how many parts of the whole are left.

We can show subtraction of fractions with a common denominator on a number line.

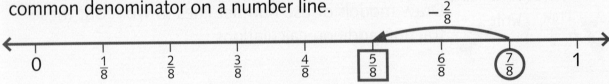

Remember to always use what you know to help work out what you don't know.

So, if we know that 7 − 2 = 5, then we also know that: $\frac{7}{8} - \frac{2}{8} = \frac{5}{8}$

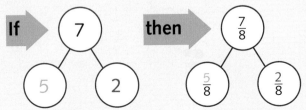

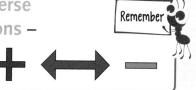

Addition and subtraction are related – they are inverse operations. That means they are opposite operations – addition reverses subtraction, and subtraction reverses addition.

Remember

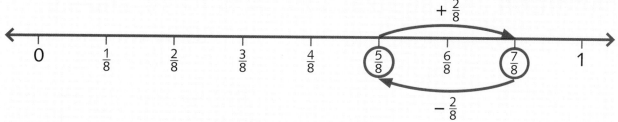

So, $\frac{5}{8} + \frac{2}{8} = \frac{7}{8}$ and $\frac{7}{8} - \frac{2}{8} = \frac{5}{8}$

If we know one fraction calculation, then we know three other related facts.

If $\frac{5}{8} + \frac{2}{8} = \frac{7}{8}$ and $\frac{2}{8} + \frac{5}{8} = \frac{7}{8}$

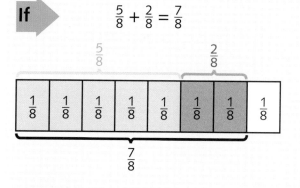
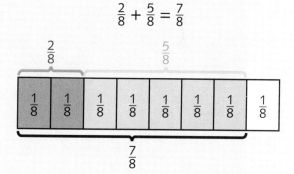

then $\frac{7}{8} - \frac{2}{8} = \frac{5}{8}$ and $\frac{7}{8} - \frac{5}{8} = \frac{2}{8}$

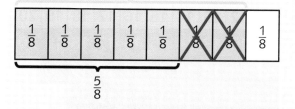

Work out these fraction calculations.

$\frac{7}{9} - \frac{3}{9} = \boxed{}$ $\frac{6}{8} - \frac{1}{8} = \frac{7}{8} - \boxed{}$

$\frac{9}{11} - \boxed{} = \frac{3}{11}$ $\frac{8}{10} - \boxed{} = \frac{6}{10} - \frac{2}{10}$

77

Addition and subtraction facts to 10 and 20

Addition can be done in any order.

So, 2 + 3 = 5 and

3 + 2 = 5

Addition is the inverse of subtraction.

So, if you know that 3 + 2 = 5

you also know that

5 − 3 = 2 and 5 − 2 = 3

+	0	1	2	3	4	5	6	7	8	9	10
0	0	1	2	3	4	5	6	7	8	9	10
1	1	2	3	4	5	6	7	8	9	10	11
2	2	3	4	5	6	7	8	9	10	11	12
3	3	4	5	6	7	8	9	10	11	12	13
4	4	5	6	7	8	9	10	11	12	13	14
5	5	6	7	8	9	10	11	12	13	14	15
6	6	7	8	9	10	11	12	13	14	15	16
7	7	8	9	10	11	12	13	14	15	16	17
8	8	9	10	11	12	13	14	15	16	17	18
9	9	10	11	12	13	14	15	16	17	18	19
10	10	11	12	13	14	15	16	17	18	19	20

+	11	12	13	14	15	16	17	18	19	20
0	11	12	13	14	15	16	17	18	19	20
1	12	13	14	15	16	17	18	19	20	
2	13	14	15	16	17	18	19	20		
3	14	15	16	17	18	19	20			
4	15	16	17	18	19	20				
5	16	17	18	19	20					
6	17	18	19	20						
7	18	19	20							
8	19	20								
9	20									

Multiples of 10 addition and subtraction facts

If you know that
6 + 8 = 14, then you
can use this to work
out facts such as:

60 + 80 = 140

Addition can be done
in any order.

So, 60 + 80 = 140

and 80 + 60 = 140

Addition is the inverse of
subtraction.
So, if you know that
60 + 80 = 140

you also know that

140 − 60 = 80
140 − 80 = 60

+	0	10	20	30	40	50	60	70	80	90	100
0	0	10	20	30	40	50	60	70	80	90	100
10	10	20	30	40	50	60	70	80	90	100	110
20	20	30	40	50	60	70	80	90	100	110	120
30	30	40	50	60	70	80	90	100	110	120	130
40	40	50	60	70	80	90	100	110	120	130	140
50	50	60	70	80	90	100	110	120	130	140	150
60	60	70	80	90	100	110	120	130	140	150	160
70	70	80	90	100	110	120	130	140	150	160	170
80	80	90	100	110	120	130	140	150	160	170	180
90	90	100	110	120	130	140	150	160	170	180	190
100	100	110	120	130	140	150	160	170	180	190	200

Multiplication and division facts

Multiplication can be done in any order.

So, 3 × 4 = 12 and

4 × 3 = 12

Multiplication is the inverse of division.

So, if you know that 3 × 4 = 12

you also know that

12 ÷ 4 = 3 and 12 ÷ 3 = 4

×	1	2	3	4	5	6	7	8	9	10	11	12
2	2	4	6	8	10	12	14	16	18	20	22	24
3	3	6	9	12	15	18	21	24	27	30	33	36
4	4	8	12	16	20	24	28	32	36	40	44	48
5	5	10	15	20	25	30	35	40	45	50	55	60
8	8	16	24	32	40	48	56	64	72	80	88	96
10	10	20	30	40	50	60	70	80	90	100	110	120

Multiples of 10 multiplication and division facts

If you know that 3 × 4 = 12, then you can use this to work out facts such as:

30 × 4 = 120 and 3 × 40 = 120

Multiplication is the inverse of division. So, if you know that 30 × 4 = 120

you also know that

120 ÷ 4 = 30 and 120 ÷ 30 = 4

×	1	2	3	4	5	6	7	8	9	10	11	12
20	20	40	60	80	100	120	140	160	180	200	220	240
30	30	60	90	120	150	180	210	240	270	300	330	360
40	40	80	120	160	200	240	280	320	360	400	440	480
50	50	100	150	200	250	300	350	400	450	500	550	600
80	80	160	240	320	400	480	560	640	720	800	880	960
100	100	200	300	400	500	600	700	800	900	1,000	1,100	1,200